Credit Check

CREDIT CHECK

Giving Credit

Where Credit Is Due

By

Charles J Thayer

Scott
your Dad was a
Great Friend for 40+ years

[signature]

Credit Check

Why the title "Credit Check"?

This book is not an autobiography – my goal is giving credit to the people that have made my business career possible. Most of my career has been related to banking and investments and banks conduct a "credit check" to make certain a potential borrower is credit worthy.

In my case, I want to "give credit where credit is due" and a title borrowed from the banking industry just seemed appropriate.

You can pick and choose any chapter or article to read. The following chapters are not necessarily in chronological order and do not need to be read in sequence.

Charles J Thayer

"Don't go around saying the world owes you a living,
The world owes you nothing,
It was here first."

Mark Twain

Dedicated to my parents,

Dr. Bruce V Thayer, DDS

Neoma Obermeyer Thayer

Table of Contents

Section II: Publications & Articles

Directors & Boards Magazine

Directors Digest

Section III: Personal Insight

Preface

"A Little Help From My Friends"
The Beatles @ 1967

This song by the Beatles was released in 1967, the year I graduated from the University of Kansas. Little did I appreciate then how true this would be over the next fifty years!

One's legacy is not based on the number of titles, board positions or deals completed – a person's legacy is only as good or bad as the relationships they have established. Many business "friends" quickly fade away when the business relationship ends; a few become personal friends for decades. This book represents my tribute to many, but not all, of the people who have helped me.

A book about business relationships by design ignores many important personal relationships. I have been very fortunate to have strong family support and words alone cannot express my love and admiration for my family. I have also enjoyed the company of many non-business friends and I thank them for introducing me to many non-business adventures.

History has a pattern of repeating itself and every generation [mine included] seems to think they are "smarter" than the older generation. Hopefully these stories help upcoming generations appreciate the value of developing relationships with mentors who are willing to share a little wisdom from their achievements and "scar tissue" from their mistakes.

I fear the availability of information on the Internet today is being viewed by many as a replacement for the need to seek advice and learn from the personal experience of other people. Wikipedia cannot replace the value of the experience and judgment you will gain from your mentors.

"Human beings, who are almost unique in having the ability to learn from the experience of others, are also remarkable for their apparent disinclination to do so."

Douglas Adams

Hitchhiker's Guide to the Galaxy

Introduction

I hope that this collection of business stories helps upcoming generations benefit from my fifty years of experience working with a wide variety of amazing people. My focus is on the positive contributions of the people identified in the following chapters – this is not an exposé, so don't expect any secrets to be disclosed.

Most of my career has been working with financial institutions. Unfortunately, as a consequence of the financial crisis [2007-2009] banks and bankers have become the piñata of the media, politicians, regulators and the general public – everyone wants to take a swipe. My concern is this negative view will discourage talented new graduates from seeking their future careers in financial services.

No economy can function without a strong financial system. Commercial banks provide a safe FDIC insured method for everyone to save, provide credit to businesses to finance new jobs, and provide credit to individuals to buy the services and products produced by our businesses. Our banking system provides the daily "oil" required for our nation's economic engine to function successfully and create new jobs for the benefit of everyone.

Investment banks [Wall Street] permit individuals to take a step beyond saving and to invest in the stocks and bonds that provide the long-term capital that is required to support the long-term growth of new businesses. Businesses like Microsoft and Apple didn't even exist when I graduated from the University of Kansas.

My imagination cannot envision the types of businesses and jobs that will exist fifty years from today.

"Opportunity Is All Around You –
Reach Out and Take It."

David & Ida Eisenhower
President Eisenhower's Parents
Abilene, Kansas

Section I

This first section contains a series of short stories describing selected business activities and the people who were important contributors to both the business events described and to my business career.

Only the first chapter provides a chronological history and the stories that follow are not necessarily presented in chronological order.

You can pick and choose any chapter to read, as these stories do not need to be read in sequence.

Charles J Thayer

Chapter One

Abilene to Palm City

My hometown, Abilene, Kansas, is a small Midwest farming community of about 6,000 people located in central Kansas. Settled in 1858, Abilene was originally a stagecoach stop and then with the coming of the railroad between 1867 and 1871, became the first of the original "Wild West" cow towns located at the end of the Chisholm Trail. Cowboys would bring longhorn cattle up from Texas to be loaded on the new railroad line and shipped east.

Abilene's best-known Marshall was Wild Bill Hickok who was known for his marksmanship and gun fighting skill. History tends to overlook the fact that while in Abilene the only person he shot and killed was his own deputy - by mistake. Abilene's days as a Wild West cow town ended in 1872 as the railroad was extended to Dodge City, the next stop at end of the Chisholm Trail.

Abilene was once again the focus of national attention during my childhood as the hometown of President Eisenhower. This small Kansas town is now a tourist destination offering tours of the Eisenhower family home, the Eisenhower Presidential Library and the Eisenhower Museum, a remarkable facility that contains exhibits of both WWII and Eisenhower's Presidential years.

My grandparents and my father were acquainted with the Eisenhower family. In the 1950's, Ellison Ketchum, Executive Director of the Eisenhower Presidential Library Commission, was a frequent guest at our home for Sunday dinners. Ketchum helped host Eisenhower's visits to Abilene. Such relationships gave our family unique insight into national events.

My sister, Linda, and I both inherited a strong work ethic from our father, Bruce, and our mother, Neoma. Born in 1904, our father experienced both the 1920's and the Great Depression. Born in 1921, our mother grew up during the Great Depression. Both of our parents were independent and self-sufficient individuals and the depression taught them nothing in life was guaranteed.

Today my sister and I realize how fortunate we were to have two wonderful parents who provided us with a solid foundation for our future. Many children are not so fortunate.

Dad was a dental surgeon and Mom worked as an assistant in his dental office. Dad was dedicated to providing the best care possible. After fifty years of practice he decided it was time to retire to South Texas in 1976. He was 72 and he did not want the quality of his work to decline as he had witnessed with other doctors in town.

I participated in football, basketball and track in my early school years but was not an outstanding athlete. Having a job as a teenager was expected and in High School I worked several days a week after school at the local drug store. I still found time to participate in school activities, including the school plays and debate. My grades were good enough for me to be accepted to the University of Kansas, but I was certainly not selected as the most likely to succeed.

For many years our family vacationed at a small lake in Minnesota. I found excitement in running the small boat that was provided with our cabin. As an avid reader and frequent visitor to our Public Library I suspect I read every book about boats on the shelves. Due to this growing fascination with boats, I decided I wanted to study to be a marine architect.

Ruth Lake, Minnesota @ Early 1950's

The merits of investment diversification were also learned during my teenage years. Although we lived in town, my high school girlfriend lived on a small "ranch" just outside of town with several horses and some cattle. After reading a book about investing in cattle, this "town" kid decided to buy a calf to feed and sell. I borrowed a little money from our local bank, attended the local cattle sale and made an arrangement with my girlfriend's father to keep the calf at their ranch.

Bad outcome – I learned early about the risk of investing on "margin" - the calf got sick and died and I still owed money to the bank. My solution was to borrow more money from the bank and buy several calves [diversification] so the future profit would cover the amount of the combined loan. Probably not smart, but it worked.

When I graduated from Abilene High School in 1962, it never occurred to me to consider a college outside of Kansas and the University of Kansas was the logical choice. However, after two years it became clear I had little design imagination and architecture of any kind would not be in my future.

"When you come to a fork in the road, take it."
Yogi Berra

We all reach a "fork in the road" from time to time and when and how we face these critical decision points will have a lasting impact on our lives. I like this quote from Yogi as it implies you must make a choice and keep moving forward, not just "run in place". This book will highlight the "forks in the road" that have determined the direction of my life and the people who influenced my career.

My first serious "fork in the road" was encountered after two years of college. Given no clear educational direction, I decided to enlist in the Navy Air Reserve rather than face the military draft. The Navy offered six months of active duty training with six years of reserve duty. Trained as an aviation electrician, I was fortunate not to be called up for additional active duty in Vietnam. For most of my tour of duty I served reserve weekends once a month at the Naval Air Station in Olathe, Kansas.

The short time I served on active duty with the Navy provided me with adequate time to reconsider my career goals. I decided to return and enroll in the Business School Program at University of Kansas. I had no desire to pursue a military career but the Navy was a great character building experience for me. Based on my experience, I suspect military training or some type of required community service might well benefit future generations. However, it's fortunate that we live in a country that offers current generations a choice about military service.

After returning to college, another student and I were presumptuous enough to start publishing an investment newsletter for regional stocks. I won the coin flip to see which name would be first and we organized the "Thayer-Mixer Company" as a registered investment advisor [easier in 1966]. We changed the name to "Business Data Research" when asked why an appliance company was publishing an investment letter!

I graduated in 1967 with a BS in Business Administration, not an MBA. Mixer graduated and moved to take a job in Florida. After graduation I recruited several of my business school professors to join me part-time so we could offer financial and marketing consulting services.

The initial focus of our consulting business was doing analysis for small community banks in Kansas and Missouri and I moved to Kansas City to help grow our business in this much larger market. Following our shift in focus to consulting, I sold the investment newsletter to a brokerage firm in Wichita, Kansas.

"80% of Success is Showing Up"
Woody Allen

I believe that "showing up" is at least 80% of both personal and business success. You never know how something you do or someone you meet will impact your future. I am not supportive of people who make the excuse that someone else was "just in the right place at the right time". Being in the right place requires showing up at the right place.

For example, one evening at the University of Kansas I attended a student business club meeting that had invited Maurice Johnson, an Executive Vice President from First National Bank, one of the largest banks in Kansas City, as a speaker.

Following the program Johnson invited the students to visit him at the bank if we were in the city. After my move to Kansas City I opened our business accounts at Johnson's bank and I made a point to keep in contact with him. Little did I know at that time how this relationship with Johnson would impact my future career.

Another important event occurred after moving to Kansas City when an intelligent and attractive young woman, Doris Van Hee, captivated my attention. Doris, a recent college graduate, managed the medical records department at a Kansas City hospital.

Our relationship flourished and Doris and I were married in 1968. Doris is a remarkable woman and I was a very fortunate young man. Doris and I were very proud parents when our son, Travis, was born the following year in Louisville, Kentucky.

However, on the business side, working with my college professors in our new consulting business encountered internal friction as our combined lack of practical experience limited our ability to grow the business. It was simply too-much too-soon and our ambitions exceeded our experience and capabilities. As a result, I resigned and Doris and I decided to move to Louisville, Kentucky to pursue our new careers.

These experiences were an early lesson in the importance of working with people who "walk the walk" not just "talk the talk".

"Choose Wisely"
Movie: Indiana Jones

This decision to resign and move followed a "fork in the road" conversation when I sought advice from a banking client in Kansas City. He asked me two questions that I still remember:

- What is my strength? – I responded, "finance".
- What is my weakness? – I responded, "marketing".

This banker replied, "I agree and suggest you find a marketing job at a financial institution; it will build on your weakness and keep you engaged in the field of your strength."

"Life is like a box of chocolates
You never know what you're gonna get"

Movie: Forrest Gump

Citizens Fidelity Bank in Louisville, the largest bank in Kentucky, had recently recruited Maurice Johnson as its new President. I shared this strength-weakness conversation with him. As a result, in early 1969, I was offered and accepted a job at Citizens as a management trainee in the bank's Marketing Department.

At that time Citizens utilized the services of a psychologist to assess if a candidate would "fit" the culture of the bank. In later years I learned this psychologist concluded I would not "fit" – fortunately Johnson's goal was to start changing the existing culture of the bank and I was invited to join the bank's training program.

Starting as a management trainee at $6,900 per year did not appear to be a very promising beginning in what was considered a rather boring and highly regulated industry. My decision to accept the job was based on my confidence and respect for Johnson.

Johnson also set the stage in 1975 for my long-term commitment to working with the Cystic Fibrosis Foundation when he asked me to stop by his office and he suggested it was time for some "community involvement". He asked if I would be interested in joining the board of a local charitable organization. A few days later he indicated the Kentucky-West Virginia Chapter of Cystic Fibrosis was interested in having a board member from Citizens.

I accepted the invitation and my 40+year involvement with the Cystic Fibrosis Foundation is described in Chapter Twelve.

Johnson also played an important role in other important events in my career. The Citizens Fidelity story is described in Chapter Three and covers the period between 1969 and 1986 during which my career progressed from a marketing trainee to Executive Vice president and Chief Financial Officer.

In many respects Johnson was "That Man Behind the Curtain". The help and guidance I received from Johnson is a remarkable example of how an outstanding mentor can silently impact your career. I am very grateful for everything he did to help me along my path at Citizens.

On the personal side, as my career advanced my growing focus was on my job with 7:00 AM to 7:00 PM days and increasing business travel, my marriage ended with Doris. It was my fault as, sad to say, my ambition exceeded my commitment to our marriage.

Doris and Travis moved to Bowling Green, Kentucky, where she accepted a teaching position at Western Kentucky University, a location that permitted me to share an ongoing relationship with Travis. A graduate of Boston College and Vanderbilt Law School, Travis now heads his own technology business in Atlanta.

I am grateful that Doris is a wonderful mother to Travis and now grandmother to our three grandchildren. Doris gets the credit for the father our son has become and we are both very proud of Travis and his family. My respect and admiration for Doris continues to grow.

In 1986, PNC Financial Corp, with corporate headquarters in Pittsburgh, Pennsylvania, acquired Citizens Fidelity. The merger created a $27 billion asset bank, the 18th largest in the nation. None of the officers at Citizens had employment contracts and my future management role was very uncertain. The acquisition by PNC presented another "fork in the road" for me as no financial institution needs two Chief Financial Officers.

However, the fact that I was designated to coordinate Citizen's integration into PNC gave me great exposure to the executive management of PNC. I was asked by PNC's Chairman & Chief Executive Officer to join PNC as Senior Vice President & Treasurer and I moved to Pittsburgh.

The PNC story in Chapter Four covers the period from the acquisition of Citizens in 1986 to my resignation as Executive Vice President in 1989.

I frequently describe my career at PNC as the "dog that caught the car" – I had an important job as one of six corporate officers on the top floor of PNC's corporate headquarters building in Pittsburgh, but my day-to-day activity had changed from being in the center of the action to a series of meetings. I had a job that many people aspired to, however, I felt isolated rather than engaged. It was time to explore a new "fork in the road".

During my banking career I had been responsible for both Citizens' and PNC's relationships with Wall Street investment firms. As a result, I had established many business and investment contacts over the years and my announcement to leave PNC resulted in numerous invitations to discuss future career alternatives.

Harry Keefe, Chairman and founder of Keefe, Bruyette and Woods [KBW] had retired from KBW in 1989. KBW was a leading investment firm specializing in financial institutions. Based on his decades of experience, Keefe was then organizing one of the first hedge funds, Keefe Partners, to invest in the securities of financial institutions.

Keefe and I had a relationship that extended back some fifteen years at the time he approached me about a potential relationship with his new hedge fund. However, I did not want to be an employee and live in New York. I suggested that we could work out an arrangement after I organized an independent firm that could also engage in other business and investment activities.

Chartwell Capital Ltd was organized in 1990 and became a fully registered investment-banking firm with NASDAQ oversight. The Chartwell story is described in more detail in Chapter Five.

Keefe invited me to serve on his new firm's advisory board and I invested in his new hedge fund, Keefe Partners. Keefe engaged Chartwell Capital to perform financial analysis and due diligence on potential investments for Keefe Partners.

Keefe became a close friend over the next decade and for many years we enjoyed spending the New Year's holiday together aboard our boats in Palm Beach. I learned a great deal from Keefe and missed his sage advice and wisdom during the 2007-2009 financial crisis, as he regrettably had passed away in 2002.

Chartwell's activities with Keefe Partners between 1990 and 2002 are described in Chapter Six.

The arrangement with Keefe Partners also provided flexibility for Chartwell to engage in a variety of other activities for other clients. Most of Chartwell's clients and activities have been related to financial institutions. However, several non-bank adventures deserve their own chapters.

In 1990, I had been asked to help an investment group with their offer to buy Sunbeam - a Pittsburgh based small appliance business currently in bankruptcy. I helped negotiate a settlement with Sunbeam's bank lenders. Following the investment group's acquisition of the company, I was asked to join Sunbeam's board of directors.

My involvement with Sunbeam definitely deserves a separate chapter and is described in more detail in Chapter Seven. The Sunbeam story also inspired the book "*Chainsaw*", written in 1999 by John A Byrne, a senior writer at Business Week.

In 1998, another investment group asked if I would be interested in joining the board of directors of CogenAmerica, an independent electric power company. This was another business being acquired out of bankruptcy. The bankruptcy court was requiring CogenAmerica to establish a special committee of independent directors to comply with the ownership regulations for electric utilities.

CogenAmerica was headquartered in Minneapolis, Minnesota, and, despite the cold winter weather; I accepted the invitation to join the board as an independent director.

The CogenAmerica story also merits a separate Chapter and is described in more detail in Chapter Nine.

In 1998, Chartwell conducted due-diligence for Keefe Partners on a potential investment in Republic Bank in St Petersburg, Florida. Keefe decided to make a significant investment in the bank's recapitalization and I was asked to join Republic's board of directors. The Republic story is described in Chapter Ten.

In 2010, Archie Brown, Chief Executive Officer [CEO] of MainSource Financial, headquartered in Indiana, contacted Chartwell about undertaking an assessment of the bank's board structure, board committee organization and board membership. Following an interview by the board's Governance Committee, Chartwell was retained to evaluate the board and its committee structure and to recommend a board member to replace the company's retiring non-executive Chairman.

Chartwell's recommendations were accepted and the following year the board's Governance Committee approached me about joining the MainSource board of directors. Based on my confidence in Brown as the CEO and the integrity of this board, I accepted and the MainSource story is covered in Chapter Eleven.

The Chartwell story continues to this day and Chartwell's activities with its banking clients over the past 26 years are described in more detail in Chapter Five.

Before we conclude this chapter I should report that my early fascination with boating has continued and for many years I enjoyed sailing a small sailboat on Kentucky's lakes and along the Ohio River in Kentucky. In 1986, my horizons expanded while still living in Kentucky and I purchased a 40-foot sailboat located in Fort Lauderdale, Florida.

Between 1986 and 1989 the sailboat was docked in Fort Lauderdale in the winter and sailed to Connecticut for the summer. I enjoyed the offshore sailing and, with crew, sailed on several of the voyages between Florida and Connecticut.

In 1987, an Englishman, Michael Nethersole, was hired to join me on a voyage to Bermuda and then he was to deliver the sailboat from Bermuda to Florida, as I planned to return to work.

Our voyage to Bermuda occurred the week of the 1987 Stock Market Crash - before the introduction of satellite telephone service.

Following our very early morning arrival in Bermuda I used local ship-to-shore marine radio to call a friend in NYC to report our safe voyage. I was informed of the disastrous market crash and learned PNC stock had declined from $50/share to the low $30s.

Nethersole overhead the conversation, as did anyone listening to their marine radio, and once we "hung up" asked, "That sounds bad, can you still afford to pay me?" My net worth had taken a significant hit and I am certain I looked it. However, I was able to reassure him I was still solvent and he would be paid.

Nethersole has been a good friend for the past thirty years and I was proud when I was named godfather of his son, John. In 2013, John joined me as crew on our new Lobster Yacht for the voyage from Rhode Island to Maine.

The arrangement with Keefe Partners did not require me to remain in New York and I began spending most of my time in Florida. Fort Lauderdale became my home in 1989 with the purchase of a waterfront townhouse with a dock for the sailboat.

My boating activities in Florida expanded my friendships into a new world of non-bankers and many of these boating related friendships continue today. One such friendship with Molly Potter became very special and after a few boating adventures of our own we were married in 2000.

Molly is an adventurous person who after attending college in Florida for two years decided it was time to sail the oceans. In 1980, she obtained the required Coast Guard license to captain boats after their purchase in Florida for delivery to their new owners in Europe and Japan.

Molly's sailing adventures in the 1980's included multiple crossings of the Atlantic, sailing from Florida to Japan, sailing the coast of India and up the Red Sea to the Mediterranean. We have a postcard Molly mailed to her parents from Djibouti, which borders Somalia, describing her escape from a military coup in Yemen. Molly's many adventures deserve a book of her own.

Following her return to college in the 1990's, Molly focused on art and she started teaching art at the Boys & Girls Club in Fort Lauderdale. Molly is committed to mentoring kids and she established an anonymous college scholarship program for four of her Boys & Girls Club students. It was a simple program that provided modest cash scholarships based on grades and all four have now graduated from college and are lifelong friends.

Our relationship has certainly expanded my horizons. Molly maintains contact with a wide range of friends that includes people from the arts community, boating community, business executives, past and present neighbors and others that defy classification. On any given day she might communicate with a hedge fund manager, a retired state Supreme Court Judge, another artist, former students and/or a gay tattoo artist. Maintaining friendships is very important to Molly and she consistently "builds bridges", she does not "burn bridges".

During our time together in Fort Lauderdale, Molly and I switched from sailing to the "dark side" and purchased a powerboat. For eighteen years we enjoyed extended cruises aboard our 50-foot pilothouse motor yacht along the east coast and cruising the Bahamas for several months each summer. Communication systems have consistently improved and working from the boat is as easy as any hotel room.

We moved to Palm City, Florida, in 2013 and now enjoy voyages aboard our new 37-foot "Lobster Yacht", a true lobster boat hull built in Maine with a custom interior. We purchased the boat in Newport, Rhode Island, cruised to Maine to have electronics installed and then to the Chesapeake to have the interior modified to meet our work and cruising requirements.

"Lobster Yacht", Brooklin Boat Yard, Brooklin, Maine @ 2013

Molly created ceramic sculpture in her own art studio in Fort Lauderdale between 2000 and 2013. Molly's art has been sold by art galleries in several states and purchased by collectors in several countries. Molly also offered after-school art classes for kids age 7 to 14 at her art studio in Fort Lauderdale.

Molly stepped up in 2014 to open our home in Palm City to Isla Lader, an exceptionally bright 14-year-old girl who attended the after-school art program at Molly's art studio in Fort Lauderdale. We were appointed as Isla's guardians in 2015. Isla provides us with her teenage view of current events and we hope we are providing her with a solid path to adulthood.

I continue to work from my home office and Molly creates new ceramic sculpture from her art studio in our new home. Art galleries in several cities continue to sell Molly's artwork.

No grandparent can ignore bragging about their grandchildren and I am blessed that Travis and his wife Megan have three wonderful children; Liam, Grace and Maggie. They have all done exceptionally well academically and are active in school sports and other school activities. Liam now attends the University of Georgia. We are very proud of each of them and I hope they gain a little insight from this book.

This concludes my personal timeline at present and the following chapters contain individual business stories highlighting specific events and the people that helped me successfully navigate the business challenges we faced together.

"I may not have gone where I intended to go,
but I think I have ended up where I needed to be."

Douglas Adams
Hitchhiker's Guide to the Galaxy

Chapter Two

An Early Business Adventure

In the early 1960's, my father invested about $2,500 to buy a few hundred shares for me in a new company, Farm & Ranch Life Insurance, which had been organized in Wichita, Kansas. This was the first stock I owned and with my newfound interest in business I followed the company closely once I returned to college from the Navy.

In 1966, the management of the insurance company got involved in a political dispute that was followed by a series of negative newspaper articles. To be fair, it was just a political dispute; the company had not violated any insurance regulations or laws.

In what can only be described as an extremely presumptuous action, I decided the negative publicity provided a reason to initiate a proxy contest for me to be elected to the board of directors of Farm & Ranch Life. Prior to announcing the proxy contest, I contacted the Kansas Insurance Commissioner, the Kansas Securities Commissioner and the Securities and Exchange Commission to make certain any action undertaken would comply with all state and federal regulations and laws.

After recruiting two successful businessmen to join this 22-year-old college student in a proxy contest, we served notice on the day of a company board meeting and simultaneously arranged newspaper coverage of our action. Several weeks passed as the company attempted to find fault with the process we had undertaken.

Once company management had determined we had followed the rules they proposed to expand the board to include the two businessmen and myself. This ended the negative publicity and we were added to the proxy for the upcoming shareholders meeting and we were elected to the board of directors in 1967.

Management's intention was to restrict our term to one year and not to nominate us to the board the following year. However, during the first year I developed a good relationship with a large shareholder and existing board member, William Graham.

Graham was nationally recognized as a very successful oil and real estate businessman. When he and his wife were married he promised her that she would live on "Easy Street" and they did. Graham had a unique house designed by a well-known architect on a ranch near Wichita and the long driveway to their home was named "Easy Street". This also served as their mail and street address.

Graham was one of a couple dozen people described in a book, "The Busy Rich". He was well traveled and had relationships with many international and national business leaders. On one occasion when we were together in his office, he received a call from Henry Ford II to discuss the purchase of an auto plant that Ford planned to close and sell. Graham purchased the plant, sold the equipment and successfully converted it to a warehouse.

I joined Citizens Fidelity Bank in Kentucky in 1969 and the fact that I was a board member of a "public" insurance company created some interesting questions. Time off to travel and attend board meetings were not always well received by my new boss in the Marketing Department. However, arrangements were always worked out. My career at Citizens Fidelity is described in the following chapter.

Farm and Ranch continued to grow and my relationship with Graham ended any plot to kick us off the board. I served as a board member until the company was acquired in 1973.

Another "fork in the road" could have been taken when Graham called me one weekend in 1974 to ask me to come to work for him in Wichita. Never a man to mince words he simply offered to double my compensation.

Although very tempting, as a I discuss in the next Chapter, I was excited by the changes I saw occurring at Citizens Fidelity following Maurice Johnson's recruitment of David Grissom as his heir apparent and Joe Rodes to head a new Investment Division. Graham's offer occurred the same week Johnson asked me if I would be interested in working in the new Investment Division and I decided to stay and work with Rodes – what turned out to be a great decision.

Chapter Three

Citizens Fidelity Bank

In 1969, I joined Citizens Fidelity Bank, the largest bank in Kentucky, as a management trainee. Citizens Fidelity was a fairly typical commercial banking organization that Maurice Johnson had been hired to expand into consumer banking. At that time, branching by Kentucky banks was limited to the bank's home county. As a result, much of my early work in the bank's Marketing Department was related to the bank's growing branch network in Jefferson County.

At one point, I was asked to forecast and budget the activity for the bank's new credit card business. I utilized a remote time-share computer system offered by a local company to program a computer based forecasting model. My program turned out to be reasonably accurate and helped establish my early reputation for building financial models.

In 1973, Johnson recruited a young local board member, David Grissom, to join the Citizens management team as his heir apparent as Chief Executive Officer [CEO]. Grissom was educated as an attorney and he was one of the founders of what is now Humana. A non-banker, Grissom, at age 34, was a revolutionary choice for such a conservative banking organization.

Joe Rodes was recruited to join Citizens shortly after Grissom came aboard. Rodes was recruited to organize a new Investment Division to include all of the banks investment activities including the bank's large Trust and Investment Department and the bank's Bond Department, which served hundreds of other banks in several states.

Rodes was another non-banker and prior to joining Citizens he managed a brokerage office in Louisville that specialized in bond underwriting and sales for a large New York investment firm. Rodes specialty was the bond market and he was a nationally recognized leader in regional bond underwriting.

Another "fork in the road" occurred in 1974 when Johnson asked me if I would like to work with Rodes and I moved from the Marketing Department into the new Investment Division.

I credit Rodes with giving me the opportunity to really learn about financial markets and investments during the many evening hours we shared together in his office at the bank discussing capital markets. Once again Johnson had opened a door for me to enter.

Asset/Liability Management

The first OPEC oil crisis hit in 1974 and interest rates were subject to greater volatility than experienced for decades. The concept of asset/liability management was just being introduced to help bankers manage interest rate risk. Grissom assigned the task of learning more about this new concept to Rodes and we began exploring the topic.

Rodes had a very inquiring mind and he always sought answers from the best sources he could identify. We began our journey by analyzing investment research reports prepared about other banks by bank investment analysts. We identified several banks and analysts to contact and visit. Two of these visits started relationships that have lasted to this day.

Citibank had a reputation for very professional financial and liquidity management and was recognized as a leader in the new arena of asset/liability management and the management of interest rate risk. Rodes arranged for us to visit with Don Howard the Chief Financial Officer of Citibank.

The analyst team at Blyth Eastman Dillon had just written a detailed report on Citibank's asset/liability management and the management of interest rate risk. Rodes arranged for us to visit with George Hacker, the investment analyst that had prepared the report.

Other contacts were also arranged but these two visits in New York provided the best insight into how we could begin to address our management of interest rate risk. Once again I utilized the time-share computer system hosted by the local computer company and designed and programmed our first asset/liability computer model based on the insight we received from these personal visits with Howard and Hacker.

I am certain today's technologically sophisticated generation will find it amusing that this program was written in the BASIC computer language using a teletype machine for remote dial-in access to the remote time-share computer. This technology was state-of-the-art in 1974.

The asset/liability model and my earlier credit card forecasting model were both based on concepts I had learned in a matrices & probabilities math class at college. I should note this was not one of my favorite classes and, despite my lack of enthusiasm at the time, it probably turned out to be my most valuable class.

Our asset/liability model was enhanced over the next ten years but the most important element was the input received from our business managers. The officers responsible for managing each sector of the bank's balance sheet updated their projections for growth and liquidity requirements every month. These updated projections were then tracked on a weekly basis for accuracy.

Our asset/liability model was tested and updated frequently by my staff to improve accuracy. But the key to accuracy was not sophisticated programming, accuracy was based on accurate input and a clear understanding of how the model worked. Several attempts by the bank Technology Division's programming staff to enhance the model didn't pass the easy-to-use and accuracy test and we adopted the following philosophy:

"Just Because a Computer Can Do It Doesn't Mean You Should Do"

Over the past twenty years asset/liability programs have become increasingly complex. I question the benefit of forecast assumptions made by bank staff that frequently replace actual management input. In addition, outside economic forecasts and assumptions frequently drive projections for growth and many interest rate scenarios are selected just to meet regulatory requirements.

In my view, if you feel a need to rely on external sources for internal management input then you don't have the right management team.

Rodes and Grissom organized an Asset/Liability Committee and the bank's senior business executives met every Thursday morning at 7:00 AM to track their actual activity with their forecast. As a result, forecasts became increasing accurate over time as our objective was accuracy and no additional credit was awarded to executives for exceeding forecast.

We also adopted a philosophy of managing interest rate risk rather than maximizing net interest income based on our interest rate forecast. Our goal was to test various interest rate forecasts and structure the bank's balance sheet to generate a steady flow of net interest income in any of our interest rate scenarios.

This philosophy served us well for the next ten years as Citizens generated steady income growth and stock price appreciation during a very volatile economic climate that included rapidly rising interest rates to over 20% followed by rapidly falling rates.

Many bankers that adopted a strategy of "taking a view on rates" and attempted to maximize income based on their interest rate forecasts experienced significant earnings and stock price volatility. Investors clearly preferred to invest in the stock of banks that managed risk to avoid excessive earnings volatility.

Rodes also encouraged me to focus on the most important factors and not get distracted by nor distract other people with information that did not have a significant impact on results. In his view, too many people try to show how intelligent they are by providing an overwhelming amount of detail and, as a result, they do not provide perspective on the topic. Both Rodes and Grissom had an ability to see through such distraction and focus on the most important issues.

> *"If you can't explain it simply,*
> *you don't understand it well enough."*
> *Albert Einstein*

These were some of the lessons that Rodes and I learned from our conversations over time with both Howard and Hacker. Rodes and Grissom wanted to maintain contact with the best people and obtain the best advice available – excellence was just expected, just like breathing you had no alternative.

In 1975, I attended the Executive Banking Program offered by Columbia University in New York. This was the first of three executive programs I attended at major universities. The program was very beneficial but I found the asset/liability class to be deficient. I was complimented when Columbia asked me to return as a faculty member the following year to teach the section on asset/liability management.

Over the next few years, I would make such presentations at a number of bank educational programs and frequently encounter "push back" from the investment mangers from banks that had established their investment portfolio as a "profit center". These managers viewed their job as maximizing income from the investment portfolio rather than managing interest rate risk to help produce steady net income for bank shareholders.

Investor Relations

In 1975, Rodes and I were assigned the task of expanding our relationships with the Wall Street investment community and potential investors. The bank's stock was traded over-the-counter and a more active market required more brokerage firms to make a market for the stock.

We identified a number of firms included Keefe, Bruyette & Woods, [KBW] a New York firm specializing in bank stocks. My relationship with the firm's Chairman & Chief Executive Officer, Harry Keefe, would prove to offer another "fork in the road" fifteen years later.

Again our path was to identify banks and other public companies that had already established investor relation programs and learn from their experience. Our contacts with Howard at Citibank and Hacker gave as an excellent start that we expanded to others based on their guidance.

As an example, we learned that a large New York based bank was supplementing their quarterly financial reports with a separate analysis prepared to help explain trends in the bank's performance to bank stock investment analysts.

Discussions with research analysts like Hacker at the investment banks we were contacting indicated they were reluctant to add a rather small bank like Citizens without much trading activity to their coverage. Analyzing any bank required a lot of work on their part to track financial performance in the format they used for their investment analysis.

Our solution was to do the "homework" for them and we initiated a quarterly "Investment Letter" to accompany our regular quarterly shareholder reports. Our Investment Letter helped introduce Citizens to new shareholders by presenting our results and trends in the format utilized by bank research analysts. We also started making quarterly visits to New York to update research analysts, shareholders and potential investors.

This approach produced significant results for Citizens as investment coverage, stock trading volume, the bank's shareholder base expanded and our stock price performed better than other regional banks. However, the most important aspect of these visits may well have been the relationships we established throughout the investment community.

Over time, our reporting and performance gained creditability and the conversations with analysts and investors shifted somewhat from discussions just about Citizens to also include discussions about the banking industry. These quarterly conversations became an invaluable source of external information that helped us navigate some very volatile financial markets.

Research analysts and investors receive an overwhelming amount of information, then and now, with financial data being reported every quarter. Our goal with the Investment Letter was to do their homework for them and make it as easy as possible to analyze and invest in Citizens Fidelity.

We also circulated the Investment Letter to our board members, all of our senior managers, made it available to all employees and we held an in-person Q&A session with all senior managers every quarter.

Strategic Planning

In 1976, I was assigned the task of strategic planning for Citizens and started reporting directly to Grissom. Once again we reached out to identify companies and people that were actively engaged in strategic planning and arranged visits with people who were experienced with the challenge.

Johnson and Rodes arranged a couple of memorable visits. The first was at Xerox, a company facing the loss of patent protection on their most important product, the plain paper copier. Their Chief Executive Officer was kind enough to host my visit with his planning team. What I learned was how difficult it was to change the culture of a company that had not previously had to face serious competition.

The second visit was with the senior financial staff at ITT, an international company noted for its financial forecasting and business controls. What became clear during this visit was the value of disciplined management reporting and consistent tracking of results.

Both these companies faced their own challenges but the insights I gained certainly helped me address the challenges we faced at Citizens. Grissom then asked me what it would require for Citizens to grow earnings per share by 15% a year, basically what if we set a goal to double income over the next five years.

Once again I programmed a computer model on the local time-share computer system to test various growth scenarios. The most challenging issue was how to control expenses during a period of high inflation and rapid personnel growth. The results indicated that if the bank continued to add people at the current rate it would not be possible to grant any salary increases and still achieve the earnings target.

On the other hand, doubling the size of the bank with the same number of people would work [raises could be granted] but this approach certainly presented a management challenge. When I discussed my calculations with Grissom he made it clear we would be up to the challenge. Doubling the size of the bank with the same number of people became our goal.

Grissom retained a consulting firm to conduct a workflow and efficiency project to right size the bank's existing staffing and implement systems to improve future staffing and operating efficiency. He established an internal Workflow Committee with me as its first Chairman to manage headcount. The process was simple: the Workflow Committee had to approve every staff replacement based on current needs and any staff increase had to be approved by Grissom.

The financial results achieved over the next five years [1978 to 1983] reflect the success of Grissom's approach. The bank increased in size from $1.0 billion to $2.7 billion and earnings increased from $12 million to $29 million. During this same period, employees increased from 1705 to 1775, an increase of only 70. The bank had achieved Grissom's goal; it had more than doubled in both size and earnings with essentially the same number of employees.

Holding headcount steady did in fact permit raises and the average compensation for bank employees had increased from $13,000 in 1978 to $21,000 in 1983. This represented an increase in average compensation of $8,000 per employee or 60% higher than in 1978.

It's also interesting to note that the number of Citizens branch locations in Jefferson County had increased from 27 to 50 between 1970 and 1978. This includes the early time period I was in the Marketing Department working to add branch locations. However, after I became Chief Financial Officer in 1977 the number of branch locations declined from 50 to 39 and the bank's market share actually increased. The focus on efficiency had created a smaller and more effective branch system.

At one point an analyst working for me came in my office with a recommendation to close an existing branch. The analyst was very critical of the location. I suggested he find the original report so we could question the research. I am not certain what his reaction really was when he discovered I did the original research and I had recommended the branch location. Ten years later he was correct and we closed the branch.

During this same period, the mix of people and jobs changed substantially as a result of new technology combined with common sense job reviews every time we had a request to replace a departing employee.

The results clearly demonstrate that the bank's efficiency improved over time with each individual decision. Once managers got the message, they made most of their own headcount reductions without submitting a request to the Workflow Committee. Careful day-to-day management produced a better paid, more efficient workforce.

In my experience, when qualified managers understand they have the responsibility and authority to make day-to-day decisions the results are very positive. Senior executives don't need to baby sit quality managers and Grissom insisted on quality people.

Chief Financial Officer

In 1977, Maurice Johnson retired and David Grissom became CEO. Grissom selected me as the bank's next Chief Financial Officer [CFO] and, at age 33, my responsibilities probably expanded beyond my existing experience and capabilities. Grissom had grown frustrated with the succession of CFO's he had recruited from major non-bank corporations during the past several years and he decided to take a risk on me.

At that time, few banks of any size had organized their accounting, asset/liability, strategic planning and related finance functions under the leadership of a Chief Financial Officer. This was a new organizational concept for banking and for Citizens.

Grissom recognized the need for me to expand my knowledge and promptly sent me to an executive program for financial executives at Harvard. This was a challenging program that clearly expanded my contacts and perspective and helped build self-confidence. The Harvard program encouraged a very competitive atmosphere and I discovered that I could compete with this group of very experienced domestic and international financial executives.

Several years later, I also attended the executive program for financial executives at Stanford. A much more cooperative atmosphere at this program also expanded my knowledge and perspective of financial management.

I continued relationships with several financial executives who also attended these two programs and the bank clearly benefited from my future visits with a couple of the international executives during my business travels in Europe. These programs were instrumental in advancing my financial education, international perspective and management skills. I recommend any new executive search out and attend the best programs available to advance their knowledge and professional relationships.

The bank's membership in the American Bankers Association also gave me the opportunity to participate in several banking schools and professional committees. These activities are described in Chapter Thirteen.

I also want to share a story that helps describe my working relationship with Grissom. I don't remember the topic but early in my role as CFO I set up a meeting with Grissom to discuss what I thought was a critical decision that required his input.

As I started to explain the problem he looked puzzled and asked me; "Does this bank have a Chief Financial Officer?" Obviously my response was "yes". He then asked who it was and I responded, "I am". Grissom responded, "This is the type of decision that a Chief Financial Officer makes so don't ever ask me to make a decision for you again."

The message was clear and, although I kept him informed of decisions I made over the years, I don't recall Grissom reversing a decision even if he would have done something differently. However, some decisions are CEO decisions and I quickly learned it is important to know the difference.

Financial Reporting

Although I took several accounting classes in college I am not a CPA and was not trained as an accountant. In fact, I never worked in the accounting department of the bank.

Financial reports for financial institutions were beginning to change in the late 1970's to reflect increasing oversight by both banking regulators and, for publicly owned banks, the Securities & Exchange Commission.

For example, new disclosures for loan loss reporting and the presentation of the loan loss reserve occurred after the 1974 failure of Franklin National Bank in New York. The failure of Franklin National was the largest bank failure at that time and was due to a combination of bad loans, inadequate loan loss reserves and a significant interest rate risk mismatch.

In our case, internal management reports, board presentations and the Investment Letter were all modified to reflect the following analytical approach used by the investment community. This income and expense presentation is standard today but it was considered quite radical at the time; I was frequently told, "That's not proper accounting".

Interest Income	Non-Interest Income
Interest Expense	Non-Interest Expense
Net Interest Income	Net Non-Interest Expense

We developed an internal pricing and cost transfer model for both the cost of funds and the cost of support services such as data processing. Our objective was to evaluate the contribution to cover overhead and profitability for each line of business and consistently improve the efficiency of all support services.

We also tried to incorporate some common sense. For example, we discontinued the allocation of the cost of in-house legal staff when it became clear that managers would not check with legal [incur internal cost] to ask questions that might avoid a potential problem. We wanted managers to check with legal and they would do so if it was "free". The legal staff could then decide if a potential issue required their legal follow-up.

An example of competitive pricing occurred when we changed the approach from cost allocation to competitive pricing for certain internal services. For example, the manager of support services had created a large centralized copy and printing center. However, when we started using the pricing of outside copy services as our internal price it became clear his approach was not cost effective.

All internal reporting was designed to educate our board and executives about the factors that impacted the performance of the bank. We did include standard financial reports for earnings but our focus was on the analysis of results.

Early Technology

Most banking systems in the 1970's were located on large IBM mainframe computer systems. However, the flexibility offered by the local time-share computer company provided the technology platform for my development of both the early credit card model and the asset/liability model.

In 1978, we purchased two TRS80 desktop computers [in later years called the "Trash 80"] and a printer from Radio Shack for the accounting department. One of the TRS80's was located in my office and the other was with the financial analysis team.

These TRS80s were the first desktop computers purchased by the bank. The TRS80s were considered game toys and were greeted with skepticism by much of the accounting and technology staff. However, skepticism dissipated once we moved the asset/liability model from the outside time-share system to the TRS80 and we could demonstrate the capability of running multiple financial simulations much faster.

The story behind the purchase of the TRS80's in 1987 and the eventual adoption of the IBM PC as standard equipment after it was introduced in 1981 is worth sharing.

During a business trip to New York in 1975 a college friend, Patricia Warner, wanted to introduce me to her fiancée, Jack Brennan. We met for drinks and dinner at the Sherry Netherland, an upscale boutique hotel. Brennan was an engineer and at that time worked for CBS television. Patricia had a sense of humor and told me that Brennan expected me to be a hick from Kansas.

Not to disappoint, I showed up at the restaurant in a business suit wearing my cowboy hat and boots. Upon arrival I turned my chair around with my arms on the back and, with a country accent, ordered a can of beer. When the waiter returned with a glass of beer I again requested a can and no glass.

Brennan was appalled, hoping no one recognized him, and Patricia was fighting to hold back laughter. After a short while the "act" was discontinued and we had an enjoyable evening that led to a long friendship.

A few years later, Brennan began his career of buying small troubled companies to turn around and sell. In 1978, I visited Brennan at a small company in New Jersey that manufactured industrial belts he had recently purchased. During the tour he told me about a recent visit he had made to Radio Shack with his young son and how he accidently discovered the TRS80, one of the first desktop computers. He had purchased several units and was using TRS80 software for both accounting and payroll.

He then took me into the sales and pricing department and demonstrated a program he had written on a TRS80 to compute bids based on technical input provided by the sales team. This new system permitted his sales team to call in the proposed bid information to the home office and the new program had reduced his bid turnaround time from several days to less than an hour.

After I returned to Louisville, I visited a Radio Shack store and had the first desktop computers delivered to the bank. The introduction of the IBM PC in 1981 gave credibility to the personal computer as a business machine, not just a toy.

Once the IBM PC was available, we set up a system that all new personal computers had to be purchased by the Data Processing Division and then "leased" to the department that wanted to use the equipment [including the accounting department]. This centralized approach prevented the uncontrolled proliferation of personal computers experienced by many organizations.

Forest Gump was right – "you never know what you're gonna get" when you visit a friend. Brennan introduced me to the benefits of using a desktop [personal] computer.

Citizens Fidelity Overview

Citizens had historically been called the "Bankers Bank" as a large number of community banks in Kentucky and surrounding states utilized Citizens as their bank for clearing deposits, purchasing bonds, servicing credit cards, etc.

At the time I became Chief Financial Officer in 1977, Citizens was about $1.0 billion in assets, the largest bank in Kentucky. For regulatory flexibility the institution was organized as a holding company, Citizens Fidelity Corporation, which owned the bank, Citizens Fidelity Bank. For simplicity I will refer to the combined organization as Citizens or the bank.

Under Johnson's leadership during the 1970's, the bank began expanding its branch network in Louisville/Jefferson County to increase its deposit base and expand consumer lending. However, Kentucky law prevented branches outside the bank's home county and consumer deposit growth was restricted.

Citizens was engaged in regional commercial lending and the bank was faced with utilizing a variety of financial instruments to fund the commercial loan growth required for earnings growth.

People like Howard stressed the need for liquidity management and we adopted a policy of direct funding with customers rather than utilize the services of Wall Street brokers. In addition, we always maintained a large pool of funds sold to other banks and other money market assets to provide liquidity in the event our access to borrowing to fund our loan portfolio was restricted.

On the funding side we centralized the sale of certificates of deposit over $100,000 [CDs] in our new "Money Center". This was a department in our Investment Division staffed by people that sold the bank's CDs to other banks, thrifts, insurance companies and other investors across the country. We wanted to "know our customers" rather than depend on brokers.

Such financial investors relied on Moody's, Standard & Poor's, Fitch and new bank credit rating firms like Keefe BankWatch and a service offered by Fox-Pitt Kelton in England. We provided financial information and made frequent visits to each of these bank credit rating firms to maintain the highest credit ratings available.

Interest rates on consumer deposits were limited at that time by Regulation Q - only large CDs over $100,000 and a few other instruments such as commercial paper could be sold with higher interest rates to our customers.

We utilized a number of these other funding instruments including repurchase agreements [Repos], commercial paper [CP] and Eurodollar certificates of deposits [E$CDs] for our customers to purchase.

Our liquidity strategy was tested when interest rates increased dramatically following the second OPEC oil crisis in 1979-1980. The entire banking and thrift industry encountered a liquidity challenge when interest rates on Treasury securities [14%+] exceeded the 5.25% interest rate ceiling on consumer deposits due to Regulation Q. As a result, bank and thrift customers nationwide began withdrawing money from their deposit accounts to purchase government bonds.

Citizens also experienced deposit withdrawals, however the bank encountered no liquidity issues as we had ample asset liquidity, solid credit ratings and direct contact with all our non-deposit funding customers. In fact, Citizens continued to be a source of liquidity for other financial institutions.

Our future business strategy was to diversify our core funding with the acquisition of community banks in and we encouraged Kentucky lawmakers to permit the acquisition of banks in other Kentucky counties. In 1984, Kentucky finally enacted legislation permitting the acquisition of banks in other Kentucky counties and, in addition, in 1986 acquisitions would be permitted nationwide on a reciprocal basis.

Citizens Fidelity Corporation acquired ten banks and assets had grown five–fold over 10 years, from $1 billion in 1977 to about $5 billion at the time of the bank's acquisition by PNC in 1986.

Next, I want to highlight several rather unique transactions that took place during my time as CFO at Citizens.

The Mellon Transaction

Economic growth and related loan growth was extremely soft in the mid 1970's following the recession created by the 1974 OPEC oil crisis. Citizens needed to achieve loan growth if the bank was to meet management's earnings expectations.

Through one of my investment contacts I learned that Mellon Bank in Pittsburgh wanted to sell some long maturity tax-exempt loans. Their tax position had changed and they would not be able to recognize this tax benefit for several years to come.

On the other hand, Citizens could utilize tax-exempt income but we had no desire to purchase long maturity assets. Working with the bank's tax professionals, we were able to structure the purchase of Mellon's tax-exempt loans with an annual "put" back to Mellon – in other words we could sell the loans back to Mellon and avoid holding a long maturity asset.

This concept worked and both Citizens and Mellon benefited from the arrangement. Shortly thereafter, Reich & Tang, a New York based money management firm, created a new tax-exempt money market fund based on this unique concept that offered their clients higher long-term rates with daily access.

Eurodollar Market

Don Howard at Citibank continued to be a resource that helped expand our participation in the financial markets. Citibank was an active international bank and Howard helped me understand the unique character of the Eurodollar deposit market.

First, it was important to understand that a Eurodollar was only a dollar dominated asset or bank account in a bank branch office outside the United States.

Second, although it was important to understand the banking laws of such offshore locations, the deposits in branches of major banks located in banking centers like London should be considered safe.

Third, banks such as Citibank actually paid higher interest rates on Eurodollar certificates of deposit [E$CDs] than they did on certificates of deposit [CDs] issued to customers in the United States. At that time, the Eurodollar market was considered to have additional "sovereign" risk and investing in international financial markets was not yet highly integrated.

We initiated a program to purchase short-term E$CDs from the London branches of selected major banks. Investing in these E$CDs provided an investment return at a rate approximately 1% higher than our domestic cost of funds.

Citizens also established an offshore branch in the Cayman Islands so we could issue E$CDs to access additional deposits and enhance our liquidity. Once we established the offshore branch, we offered E$CDs at a slightly higher rate to our domestic customers but at a rate significantly lower than the offshore rates required by offshore investors.

The Eurodollar market has now changed and domestic and offshore rates are essentially identical so this arbitrage opportunity only existed for a couple of years about the time of the second OPEC oil crisis in the late 1970's. However, thanks to Howard, this international investment program provided several million dollars of additional net income for Citizens.

Citizens Fidelity (Ohio): The Non-Bank Bank

Kentucky had a usury law that limited the interest rate a bank could charge on consumer loans, including credit cards. As interest rates increased in the late 1970's and early 1980's the cost of funding the bank's credit card portfolio became a significant drag on earnings.

A number of national banks moved their credit card operations to either Delaware or South Dakota to avoid usury restrictions. Kentucky law limited our options but we decided to explore moving our credit card business to Ohio.

Citizens had a long history of providing services to smaller community banks in Kentucky and surrounding states. As a result, Citizens had computer systems to service credit cards for dozens of other banks across the country.

At that time, Kentucky law prevented Citizens from owning another "commercial" bank in another state. However, federal banking regulations provided an opportunity to obtain a bank charter for a new credit card bank that would not be considered a "commercial" bank under Kentucky law – a "non-bank" bank.

Martha Ziskind in our legal department was recruited to explore if Citizens could obtain such a bank charter. Ziskind was skeptical but accepted the challenge. Our approach was to form a new subsidiary bank with a national charter from the Comptroller of the Currency.

The new bank would only make credit card loans and would not make commercial loans. We believed the Federal Reserve should consider our new bank a "non-bank" for regulatory purposes and, therefore, permit the holding company, Citizens Fidelity Corporation, to own this financial institution in another state.

Ziskind did the legal and regulatory homework and we travelled together to Washington, DC, to make our case to the Chief Counsel of the Federal Reserve Bank. Due to her efforts, we successfully navigated the very complex maze of state and federal banking laws and regulations and Citizens Fidelity (Ohio) became a reality in 1983.

Ziskind would frequently "roll her eyes" when asked but was always willing to tackle a new concept or idea. She was also instrumental in the formation of the holding company's commercial paper program and the bank's offshore funding branch in the Cayman Islands. Ziskind was a great help to me and she contributed greatly to the success of Citizens.

Private Placement of Public Equity

As mentioned earlier, George Hacker had provided valuable insight on asset/liability management and I had maintained regular visits with him during my quarterly visits with investment analysts in New York. Hacker relocated to London, England, in the late 1970's and had become co-manager of Bear Stearns Europe.

Hacker invited me to make a short investment presentation about Citizens to a group of his clients while I was on a personal vacation to Europe in the late 1970's. The response to my presentation was positive and several clients were interested in expanding their investments in the United States and they began purchasing shares of Citizens.

This initial presentation convinced Hacker it was worthwhile to host annual visits by Grissom and myself to meet and discuss Citizens with additional clients. Over time, we would develop relationships with a significant number of international investors who would collectively own about 25% of Citizens outstanding common stock.

On one such visit in late 1980, the response to our presentations was so positive that Hacker suggested we consider the issuance of new shares to meet investor demand. We were interested in doing so as we wanted to raise additional capital in anticipation of a change in Kentucky law that would permit Citizens to start acquiring other banks throughout Kentucky.

However, we had a problem called preemptive rights. Citizens had to request shareholder approval to sell more shares and this process would take time, require public disclosure and require a special shareholders meeting. Preemptive rights made Hacker's suggestion impractical – but still appealing.

At that time, Citizens had an active mortgage business that utilized the forward sale of its mortgage loan production as a method of hedging its interest rate risk. In fact, while at the Stanford Financial Program I had discussed a potential program with a European investor utilizing futures and forwards to hedge their investments in mortgage securities that they were funding with foreign currency.

Hacker and I decided to explore the idea of selling Citizens shares forward for delivery after a special shareholders meeting. This approach would let Citizens sell shares in January 1981 at January's stock price subject to Citizens shareholder approval at a special shareholders meeting to be held in February. The buyer's would then have an obligation to purchase the shares at January's price at a date we selected after our shareholders meeting.

The shares would be sold as a private placement and Citizens would have an obligation to register the shares with the Securities & Exchange Commission so, once purchased, the buyers would own shares that could be traded on a stock exchange.

Stewart Conner, at that time a young banking lawyer at Wyatt, Tarrant & Combs in Louisville, was retained to research the concept and work out the details for this unique approach. Conner did the homework, and although he could find no precedent, he prepared the documents and we were in a position to move forward.

I quietly arranged travel to London and took a taxi from the airport. Given all our attempts at strict confidentiality I was shocked when the London cab driver said "welcome back sir" as we were driving to Hacker's residence – I had the same cab driver as my previous visit a few months earlier and he remembered driving me to Hacker's address! I certainly wouldn't make a good secret agent.

Hacker and I began a series of meetings in January 1981 with potential investors. Our unique approach required substantial investor education but we obtained the required commitments and I returned to Kentucky to announce a successful stock offering.

The real winners over time were Hacker and Bear Stearns as Hacker utilized this "Citizens Concept" during the 1980's to place shares for a number of other companies.

I question if Hacker and I "invented" anything but financial publications in both New York and London reported this transaction to be the first forward placement of common stock. As a result, I was somewhat amused during a presentation made by a boutique investment firm headquartered in Los Angeles in 2008 when they claimed to have "invented" this concept in the early 1990's, some 10 years after our initial transaction.

Citizens successfully completed two other capital transactions with international investors. We issued convertible debentures to investors in London in 1985 and a corporate bond issue to Japanese investors in 1986.

In hindsight it's interesting to note that Citizens undertook no capital issues in the United States - every capital transaction by this Kentucky bank was completed with international investors on more favorable terms than available from domestic investors.

All of these capital issues at Citizens were the result of working with the brightest people we could identify – nothing would have been accomplished without the help and insight of people like Hacker. It was clearly beneficial for us to expand our horizons.

Acquisition Strategy

Kentucky banking law changed in 1984 and we began a series of acquisitions that when combined with internal growth, would take the bank from about $1.0 billion in assets at the time I became CFO in 1977 to about $5.0 billion in assets at the time we were acquired by PNC in 1986.

The Bank's acquisition team consisted of Michael Harreld at Citizens, Steward Conner from the bank's law firm, Wyatt, Tarrant & Combs and analysts from my staff. Again we reached out and sought the best advice and insight we could from other banks that were successfully acquiring other community banking organizations.

In 1982, Beverly Taylor, the manager of my financial analysis team at Citizens hired Vince Berta as an analyst. Taylor had superb "people insight" and my philosophy was to give managers the authority to hire their own staff. Managers would sink or swim with their decisions and I only requested the opportunity to meet potential employees before they started work.

When Taylor asked me what I thought of Berta after our initial introduction I responded, "Are you sure?" She was and Berta was not only an outstanding analyst, he became a great future executive and a long-term friend and associate. Lesson learned: trust your people.

Grissom also recognized Taylor's ability and she was promoted to manage the bank's Audit Department and reported directly to Grissom. At that time, I selected Berta to manage the financial analysis team and he assumed responsibility for both acquisition analysis and working with the bank's Asset/Liability Committee.

Again, the contacts we had all made over the years gave us access to some incredibly helpful people. As a result, I believe we were able to avoid many early mistakes and most of our acquisitions were integrated successfully and performed as we expected.

Due diligence teams for credit and operational analysis were assembled and trained at Citizens so we would be prepared when Kentucky law was changed to permit acquisitions. We learned early that the most important issue is dealing with the people at the acquired institution. Most acquirors are too arrogant and don't recognize the importance of key people and their customers after the acquisition.

Grissom wanted to make certain our teams understood how people at the acquired institutions would "feel" and he asked me to assemble our team and conduct the following exercise.

Once the acquisition team was assembled and the members were excited by the prospect of Citizens making its first acquisition I broke the "news" that, surprise, we had accepted an offer to be acquired by a larger out-of-state bank.

I still remember the shocked looks and the level of anxiety in that room. I announced that their jobs would now be to interface with the acquiring bank's acquisition team and went around the table with instructions. After a pause I asked, "How do you feel?"

The anxiety level disappeared somewhat after I revealed the truth; this was only an exercise to help them appreciate the reaction of the people they would encounter when we made acquisitions. This exercise clearly made an early impression but I suspect it dissipated over time – until Citizens was acquired by PNC.

Financial Results

The acquisition of Citizens by PNC was negotiated and announced mid-year 1986 and completed in early 1987.

Earnings per share and dividends per share had both doubled between 1981 and 1986, a compound annual growth rate of about 15% for the five-year period prior to the acquisition by PNC. This financial track record was achieved with disciplined internal growth combined with selective acquisitions.

In my opinion, Citizens' successful acquisition program was due as much to the banks we declined to buy as banks we did buy. Successful acquisition programs also require the discipline to say "no".

The following table summarizes Citizens Fidelity's financial results between 1977 and 1986.

Citizens Fidelity Corporation	1977	1986
Year-End Assets	$ 1.0 Billion	$ 5.0 Billion
Year-End Equity Capital	$ 85 million	$ 350 Million
Year-End Total Capital [a]	$ 85 Million	$ 406 Million
Annual Earnings	$11 Million	$ 50 Million
Return on Avg Equity	13.5%	19.3%

[a] Includes $26 Million Convertible Debentures & $30 Million Long-Term Debt

David Grissom & Management Philosophy

Grissom was committed to building a management team with the best talent and the bank's senior management ranks became a blend of new and existing people in the late 1970's. The result was a senior management team consisting of intelligent and competitive individuals with a blend of banking experience. However, Grissom had no tolerance for internal politics and he required our efforts to be focused on building our business, not competing with one another. Once the new team was in place we had little turnover.

The incentive compensation plan that Grissom adopted was an important component of building this team approach. The top dozen or so executives all participated as a team in a plan that was linked to overall corporate performance; earnings per share and return on equity. Individual payout ratios for senior executives were not linked to individual performance.

The annual cash bonus was calculated as a percentage of each executive's annual salary so the actual amounts would vary to reflect each executive's job compensation but the percentage payout for each executive was identical.

Grissom also introduced stock options as a component of the executive compensation plan. Each level of our executive management team would receive the same number of options to purchase shares and the number of options awarded was based on corporate performance.

The objective was to help individual executives focus on how the team could work together to achieve our corporate goals and to think like shareholders by participating in share ownership.

Divisions of the bank, such as mortgage production, had economic cycles that would vary from year-to-year but the executive in charge would participate in the corporate plan as a team member. The management team understood that if an executive was not managing their business effectively, then it was a question of continued employment, not reduced bonus payout, and the executive would be replaced.

One other element of the executive plan was the inclusion of key staff positions such as audit, credit, legal and human resources. Grissom recognized that an effective banking operation required effective checks and balances to manage risk.

Grissom also had a surprising sense of humor. On one occasion after a long day of meetings with investors and analysts in New York I had scheduled a late meeting with a small Switzerland based investment boutique with an office in New York. I did not know the people but they had called a few days before requesting information. At that time, I indicated "I" not "we" would be in New York and I would be happy to stop by at the end of the day.

Grissom decided to join me and as we entered their office he took the lead and, to my surprise, introduced himself as Charles Thayer the CFO and introduced me as David Grissom the CEO. The meeting went smoothly as we were able exchange roles [temporarily] and we departed. On the elevator after the meeting I asked, "Why did you decide to do that?" He responded, "I always wanted to know what it was like to be the CFO".

After we returned to Louisville I received a call from the investment manager at the boutique firm indicating they had decided to invest.

Concerned about what we had done I disclosed the switch that had occurred. He just laughed and said they had figured it out – "your pictures are in the Citizens annual report". They had decided to invest because they were impressed that if we could pull off that switch we clearly understood our business.

Grissom did not pull the switch again and I was never certain if he did the switch just to test my reaction.

The banking laws changed in 1986 to permit nationwide banking. As a result, in early 1986, we decided it was time for Citizens to more actively explore an affiliation with a larger bank and the acquisition of Citizens Fidelity by PNC Financial is discussed the following chapter.

The Value of Early Mentors

Maurice D S Johnson [1912-2000]

In retrospect, Johnson opened more doors for me than I appreciated at the time. Johnson's name appears in multiple chapters of this book. He was a master of "behind the curtain" guidance and I don't recall that he ever took any credit for helping my career.

Johnson was always available to visit when I would stop by his office at First National Bank in Kansas City. He always expressed interest in our business activities and introduced me to a number of business people in Kansas City.

I suspect Johnson was responsible for waiving aside the results of the psychologist's report indicating I would not "fit" the bank's culture. He was also the reason I was invited to join Citizens Fidelity's training program.

Rodes told me after we had worked together for several years that Johnson had suggested that Rodes ask me to join the new Investment Division. However, as we talked about the process, it become clear that Johnson had talked to me first. Johnson had arranged our meetings so we would think that working together was our idea – Johnson had orchestrated the entire process.

My forty-year history with the Cystic Fibrosis Foundation started when Johnson asked if I would be interested in joining the board of a charitable organization. He called me about a week later and indicated he had identified an organization that might interest me. Some time later I learned that an executive from another local bank had already approached Johnson about having someone from Citizens join the Cystic Fibrosis board – once again he arranged the process so it appeared to be my idea, not his.

After Johnson retired as CEO of Citizens in 1977 he became a senior consultant with Arthur D Little, a national consulting firm based in Boston. In 1981, the firm published "*The Bank Directors Handbook*" and I was invited to co-author the chapter on Asset/Liability Management with Johnson. I was the only person listed on the author's page that did not work for the consulting firm.

Joe M Rodes [1931-2006]

Working with Rodes provided an amazing education for me. He was very experienced and always willing to share information about the financial markets. I not only learned from Rodes during our many after work discussions but I learned the value of searching out answers to questions from the very best people you could contact. Visits with Rodes were both exhilarating and exhausting as he made my mind work overtime.

Rodes was responsible for introductions to Howard, Hacker and Keefe. Each of these people played an important role in my future career.

The Wall Street that Rodes introduced me to in the 1970's was an era when trades were verbal and "your word" was the most important attribute you possessed. The introduction of computerized trading systems and the computer keyboard has certainly changed the value of personal relationships.

As an example, based on Rodes experience and relationships, Citizens had structured a complex bond refunding for the Kentucky Turnpike Authority that required certain firms, including Merrill Lynch in New York, to sell bonds at a fixed price in the future [a forward agreement] to a designated account.

We had a problem when it came time to finalize the bond refunding. The broker at Merrill Lynch who had approved the transaction had taken a job at another firm and, at that time, no accounting systems existed for recording such a transaction. As a result, Merrill Lynch said they had no record of this commitment.

It was my job to complete the transaction and I arranged a meeting with the in-house legal counsel at Merrill Lynch in New York to explain the transaction. After our discussion, the legal counsel indicated he would "look into it" and get back to me at a later date.

We needed to close the transaction promptly and have Merrill Lynch honor their broker's commitment, so rather than leave his office, I moved to a comfortable chair, picked up a magazine and said, "I'll wait". A short while later he returned to his office and I was informed they would honor the transaction.

We both understood the issue was acknowledging and then honoring a verbal commitment – that's the way business was done. Your word was your commitment, period.

Rodes didn't pretend to know the answers and we learned about asset/liability management together. Our discussions about interest rate risk and liquidity became the platform of my experience and philosophy over the years. All my steps forward to CFO were accompanied by Rodes.

I could visit with Rodes anytime and in his own way he always helped me gain additional insight. He retired as President of Citizens in 1979 and in later years was Chairman of the Brown Foundation in Louisville. The Foundation's office was located in the same building as one of Chartwell's banking clients and I continued to enjoy the opportunity to stop by and visit with Rodes and, as always, I departed with new insight.

Chapter Four

PNC Financial

Grissom and I consistently reviewed the bank's "strategic alternatives" and evaluated both potential acquisitions by Citizens and potential acquirors of Citizens. The banking laws had changed in 1986 to permit nationwide banking and Grissom had also established personal relationships with the Chief Executive Officer's [CEO] of potential acquisition partners.

In early 1986, we decided it was time to more actively explore an affiliation with a larger bank as a number of out-of-state financial institutions had begun expressing an interest in acquiring Citizens.

Our interest began to focus on PNC Financial with headquarters in Pittsburgh, Pennsylvania, as PNC's business model appeared to be most compatible with Citizens. Both banks were primarily commercial banks growing by acquisition, combined with strong organic growth and an expanding consumer business.

A "merger of equals" between Pittsburgh National Bank and Provident National Bank in Philadelphia had created PNC in 1982. It was the largest bank merger in American History at that time. Using PNC, the identical initials of both banks, to name the holding company was a diplomatic way of not designating the dominant institution.

Citizens would be the third major bank addition to the PNC network and the asset size of PNC increased from about $19 billion in 1985 to $27 billion at year-end 1986. However, PNC was a decentralized organization and financial reporting was the only function fully centralized and consolidated at the holding company headquarters in Pittsburgh.

On the other hand, Citizens had centralized and consolidated all significant operating and support functions to maximize operating, funding and financial efficiency. I was designated as the executive in charge of integrating operations between Citizens and PNC on behalf of Citizens, a task that focused largely on organizing systems for management and financial reporting.

This integration planning also began addressing the question of coordinating funding, liquidity and asset/liability management. The CEO of PNC determined that it was time to centralize management of these functions and he offered me a new position as Senior Vice President & Treasurer of PNC. I accepted and relocated to Pittsburgh.

As Treasurer my responsibility also included relationships with Wall Street investors and I introduced an "Investment Letter" for PNC, similar to the quarterly letter we had been publishing at Citizens. Many of Citizens' European shareholders had elected to exchange their shares in Citizens for PNC shares in the acquisition transaction. As a result, Hacker invited PNC's CEO and myself to make a series of investor presentations in London.

Shortly after my arrival in Pittsburgh the CEO announced PNC's Chief Financial Officer would be taking early retirement and another executive and myself were both elected Executive Vice President [EVP] by the PNC board of directors.

As EVP-Finance my expanded role included corporate treasury, merger and acquisition activity, investor relations, strategic planning, corporate insurance and PNC's capital markets activity conducted by PNC Securities Corp.

My initial role at PNC was certainly challenging as developing centralized funding, liquidity and asset/liability management functions was much like "herding cats" as no one wanted to give up control at the subsidiary bank level. However, with the assistance of people like Joe Irwin at Pittsburgh National Bank we were able to accomplish the task.

Irwin proved to be a valuable resource for me and was a unique individual who would put PNC's interests above his personal interest, unlike many other PNC executives. PNC had not developed the same team approach we had achieved at Citizens.

For example, at one point I was assigned executive responsibility for PNC's money-losing payroll processing business. The assignment was to fix it or sell it if possible.

The analysis completed by my financial staff clearly indicated we had an extremely high cost structure in a business with very competitive pricing. The only solution was to improved efficiency with cost reductions if this business was to operate profitably. So, could this business operate more efficiently?

During a meeting with the executive in charge we discussed the alternatives; operate more efficiently or sell the business. I was shocked when he said, "We can't sell the business, nobody would hire our employees". He revealed that for the bank to avoid terminating people he had been staffing the business with poor performers being transferred from other banking divisions.

Unfortunately, it became clear we would need to replace most of his employees if the business was to operate efficiently and return to profitability. As a result, we decided to sell the customers to a national payroll processing company and close down the business.

This executive's inability to insist on quality people and manage the business efficiently on a day-to-day basis had created a no-win situation. A sad outcome for employees who had been placed in jobs they were not equipped to perform.

PNC's capital markets business was a much more successful venture. PNC had an excellent reputation in the investment markets for tax-exempt underwriting and securities sales. However, the business was not consistently profitable. I was assigned executive responsibility for PNC's capital markets business when I was elected EVP.

PNC had recently completed a new trading floor with up-to-date electronics; however, the underwriting and sales structure was disorganized. My first step was to interview every employee to obtain a comprehensive view of people and skills. It became clear we had some excellent people in the group but a serious leadership problem.

This was my most enjoyable assignment at PNC, and I began spending most of my time each day in my "temporary" office next to the trading floor.

Working from my temporary office on the trading floor provided much easier access for all my staff, as my office on the executive floor required the use of a private elevator and passing through two levels of security. I was much more engaged with everyone at this office on the trading floor.

We had an individual in the investment group that, in my opinion, was capable of managing the sales staff if provided proper authority and support. This proved to be the case and working together we were able to attract several additional excellent sales people from other institutions in Pittsburgh.

The underwriting group was more difficult. The individual in charge seemed to know what he was doing but was a very poor manager. The solution was to remove this individual from day-to-day management and limit his activity to selected accounts. Leadership was then placed with a very capable young man in the group. Although this was an awkward arrangement on occasion, with careful oversight it was very successful.

Sales and profitability accelerated once we had the combined team in place and in 1988 PNC Capital Markets was nationally ranked for the first time as a top ten underwriter for the issuance of bonds for both health care and educational institutions.

However, my direct management role was intended to be temporary. We recruited an experienced individual from a Wall Street firm to manage PNC's capital markets business and he moved into my temporary office. As a result, I returned full-time to my executive suite on the top floor.

During this period PNC remained an active acquiror with major expansion into Delaware and Ohio. The combination of internal growth and acquisitions increased PNC's asset size from about $19 Billion in 1985, prior to the Citizens acquisition in 1986, to about $40 billion in assets in 1989.

Most important, profitability and earnings per share increased from $3.35 per share in 1985 to $5.09 in 1988 and PNC's market capitalization was ranked #4, higher than PNC's new asset ranking of #11 among all financial institutions.

Despite this success, in 1989, I became increasingly frustrated with an executive level job at corporate headquarters that was removed from the day-to-day action on the trading floor and consisted mostly of meetings. In many respects I was the "dog that caught the car" - I had a high level executive job on the top floor of PNC headquarters that appeared ideal but was no longer enjoyable.

"The dog that caught the car"

As a result, I elected to explore a new "fork in the road" and started discussing my resignation with PNC's CEO. Over the next several months we discussed alternatives for reorganization and succession and eventually announced my resignation.

Grissom had been elected as Vice Chairman of PNC with regional management responsibility following PNC's acquisition of Citizens. Grissom was a great CEO but a frustrated regional executive and he had announced his departure in late 1988. No question, I had enormous respect for Grissom and his departure no doubt played a part in my decision.

Grissom remained in Louisville and went on to organize his own investment firm, Mayfair Capital. He has served on numerous corporate boards and he is Chairman of Glenview Trust, one of the largest money management firms in Kentucky.

Although we discussed working together several times over the past twenty-six years we never discovered an appropriate venture. We remain in contact and arrange to meet for breakfast or lunch. Grissom is an amazing individual and our fifteen years of working together was a relationship that provided me with enormous professional growth – working with Grissom was certainly an exciting time.

"Twenty years from now you will be more disappointed by the things you didn't do than by the ones you did do."

"So throw off the bowline,

Sail away from the safe harbor,

Catch the trade winds in you sails,

Explore – Dream – Discover."

Mark Twain

Chapter Five

Chartwell Capital Ltd

I had no immediate career plans after resigning from PNC in 1989 as my focus had been on insuring a smooth management transition at PNC.

My near term objective was to spend some time on my sailboat and consider a number of possible options. An executive search firm attempted to interest me in another bank and Don Howard [recently recruited by Warren Buffet to be CFO of Salomon Brothers investment bank in New York] introduced me to a London based investment banking firm searching for an executive to manage their New York operation. Investment analysts had numerous suggestions and a couple of New York investment banks inquired if I would be interested in joining their firms. Although each of these alternatives was interesting, I had no desire to work for another large bank or to live and work in New York City.

Harry Keefe had approached me about working with him in some capacity at the new hedge fund he had recently organized to invest in financial institutions. My relationship with Keefe extended back some fifteen years and I had enormous respect for Keefe. However, I did not want to work in New York and suggested that we could work out an arrangement after I organized an independent firm that could also engage in other business and investment activities.

In 1990, I contacted Stewart Conner, now Managing Partner, at the Wyatt law firm in Louisville and he helped me organize Chartwell Capital Ltd as a fully registered investment-banking firm with NASDAQ oversight.

Keefe invited me to serve on his new firm's advisory board and I invested in his new hedge fund, Keefe Partners. Chartwell was engaged to perform financial analysis and due diligence on potential investments for Keefe Partners. Chartwell's relationship with Keefe between 1990 and 2002 is covered in Chapter Six.

When I organized Chartwell, I wanted to see if I could actually develop a business without building a staff. My original goal was to work from a "home office" and utilize improving technology for market information and to communicate with potential clients.

A rather heavy "laptop" computer, fax machine, an early business channel on TV and a portable cell phone the size of a book provided the technology I needed to start. In addition, I added a "car" cell phone to the sailboat that actually worked in both the USA and the Bahamas.

Learning to manage my own schedule was a serious challenge as my excellent executive assistants had spoiled me at both Citizens and PNC. I always wanted to get an early start and both Cheri Collins at Citizens and Bernadette Cattau at PNC agreed to start work at 7:00 AM to accommodate my schedule.

My daily habit at the banks was to start at 7:00 AM and stay at the office until about 7:00 PM to wrap up any outstanding items and distribute notes to my staff with my feedback on current projects. My staff soon learned to look on their desk chairs for my notes when they arrived at work in the morning.

My day still starts with a review of overnight business news from global markets. The new habits I developed to accommodate work from my new home office present a different challenge today. At the banks I seldom took work home as I would complete my work at the office and depart for dinner.

When you work from a home office, the work is always available. Today, I find it easy to work even longer hours when faced with a challenging project or assignment. Working from home certainly requires a different discipline than working from an office building. I find it convenient to work rather than finding golf or fishing to be an easy distraction – I don't play golf or fish.

In addition, today's technology provides 24-hour availability with text, email, mobile phones and Internet access. I have found learning to "turn off" is not easy – even when we are away on our new boat I find it easy to stay engaged.

However, I adjusted and for the past twenty-six years have managed to conduct business without adding permanent staff. As described in this chapter, I do team up with business associates from time to time to provide clients with quality work. In addition, I have found working with the staff support provided by my clients to be very beneficial.

Most of Chartwell's early assignments originated as a result of the personal relationships established with other bankers during my career at Citizens and PNC. I have also found relationships with law firms of all sizes to be a good source of referrals as law firms limit their practice to legal matters. I have not found accounting firms to be a source of business as their business models frequently include consulting services and accounting firms attempt to keep all business "in house".

People who are thinking about starting a bank advisory business frequently ask me for marketing advice. Frankly, I don't know what to say; my business has been based completely on personal relationships and I have not done any formal marketing.

The downside of this approach is "generational shift". Most of my early personal relationships were with people that have now retired and are no longer active in business. As a result, most of Chartwell's business today is with "second generation", people I came to know while working with my "first generation" contacts. In some cases I am now working with "third generation".

This generational shift demonstrates why quality work is required to build strong personal relationships. My goal has always been to try and identify realistic alternatives to help my clients manage risk and help them select the best path forward for their situation. Every board and management team is unique with different skills and experience and these are the people, not advisors or consultants, which provide day-to-day leadership.

In my opinion, the "cookie cutter" approach used by many consulting firms to address problems just creates a situation where the client is "told" what to do without real "ownership". The result is frequently a need for additional "follow-up" by the consulting firm.

In addition, too many consultants and investment bankers appear to be "fee driven" and their advice targets the highest fee. For example, my strategic analysis for clients does not always result in a recommendation to "sell" – a recommendation that would generate the highest fee.

My goal is to help my clients identify and select the path to produce the best long-term value for shareholders and have them take "ownership" of the result. Success is when a client doesn't call me back to solve the same problem twice.

My favorite clients are those that ask for strategic advice to grow their business, manage risk and avoid significant problems.

"[Decisions] are not generally one road or another but the possibility of many different paths. If the choice were easy then the correct road would be clear. When the choices are difficult and the way ahead is marked by twists and turns then each step ahead is marked by opportunity, uncertainty and danger."

Mark Grant: "Out of the Box"

Grant, a former neighbor and frequent guest on CNBC and Bloomberg, writes "Out of the Box" a daily email for his institutional investment clients. Sometimes, when facing a difficult situation with a client, I need to remind myself that if it were easy they would not have called me.

Chartwell's clients have been located in states across the country; Tennessee, Arkansas, Arizona, Ohio, Missouri, Texas, California, Georgia, Louisiana, Indiana, Florida, Washington, Pennsylvania, New York and Kentucky. Each of Chartwell's banking assignments has been unique. Chartwell has been engaged to provide a wide range of advice to financial institutions, corporate clients and institutional investors.

Chartwell's relationship with the investment group that acquired Sunbeam out of bankruptcy deserves a separate chapter and the Sunbeam story is covered in Chapter Seven.

The following stories describe a few of Chartwell's relationships and the people that contributed to successful outcomes over the past twenty-six years:

Tennessee: First American

In the early 1990's, Chartwell was approached by Jimmy Smith, interim Chief Executive Officer [CEO] of First American, a bank with about $6.0 billion in assets headquartered in Nashville, Tennessee. The bank was operating under a regulatory order that required a special committee of the board to oversee operations. This special committee retained Chartwell as its advisor and I worked closely with Smith, a former banker, director of the bank and member of the special committee.

This was one of Chartwell's first assignments to help a board with problem resolution and help guide the turnaround of a troubled institution. The bank was fortunate to have a quality former bank CEO on its board that could serve as its interim CEO.

Much of Smith's management team assumed that once the credit problems were resolved the bank would return to acceptable profitability. Our analysis indicated this was not the case. The bank's failure to successfully integrate its recent acquisitions had also created a very inefficient operation.

An interesting encounter occurred with the manager of the bank's investment department who was claiming he had found a way to "make money by trading bonds with Salomon Brothers", a very successful New York bond trading firm.

Needless to say, I was a little skeptical and a little investigation uncovered the fact that he had convinced the bank's accounting department that he was trading with "free" money - he was not being charged a cost of funds. This obviously produced a situation that would almost always show an accounting "profit".

It was clear Salomon was making money at the expense of the bank once we considered the cost of funds and the commissions the bank was paying to Salomon. When it's too good to be true……….

Under Smith's leadership the bank was returned to solid footing and at the conclusion of this yearlong assignment, the bank was able to successfully recruit a new CEO.

Arkansas: First Commercial

First Commercial was a bank with about $1.0 billion in assets headquartered in Little Rock, Arkansas. In the early 1990's, the bank's CEO approached Chartwell about helping the financial staff upgrade financial reporting, asset/liability management and financial controls. This initial assignment was followed by working with the CEO and the board on strategic planning for the institution.

This relationship produced an unexpected side story. While I was doing some due diligence for Keefe Partners at another institution in New Orleans, an executive assistant interrupted our meeting and indicated I had a phone call. We were busy and I said, "please take a message and I will return the call". The executive assistant replied, "I think you will want to take this call, it's from the White House".

Surprised, I stepped out of the conference room to the amazed look of the other people. In fact, it was from the head of President Clinton's transition team, who happened to be a member of the Arkansas bank's board. He was calling for a reference on a candidate for a Treasury Department position. The request was confidential so I could not disclose the nature of the call but it certainly elevated my stature that day.

California: Silicon Valley

Chartwell was approached by an investor who was concerned about the declining performance of Silicon Valley Bank, a $1.0 billion asset bank in California. The bank's CEO and board of directors were receptive to working with Chartwell and retained Chartwell to conduct an assessment. The bank had been a high performer in the early 1990's but had recently encountered credit problems.

Chartwell's assessment indicated the bank's CEO had deviated from the bank's core commercial banking strategy and had started making real estate loans to invest excess liquidity without having established an adequate credit and support system.

The CEO's philosophy had been, "Why worry - California real estate never goes down in value". Once again, history repeated itself, values had declined and unprepared banks were again incurring significant losses.

It became clear to the board that the bank would require new leadership and Chartwell worked with an executive search firm to help the board identify a new CEO. This was an early example of a board that understood its responsibilities and took decisive action. The results over the past several decades have been impressive and Silicon Valley Bank has grown to $40 billion in assets as of 2016.

Kentucky: Bank of Louisville

Bertram Klein, Chairman & CEO of Bank of Louisville in Kentucky, contacted Chartwell about providing guidance for the bank's growing financial department. The bank had a quality financial staff but they lacked executive experience. The bank's financial staff responded positively and a solid long-term relationship was established with the staff, the CEO and the board of directors.

Klein insisted on "bad news first" in his staff meetings, a discipline he consistently enforced that helped him avoid surprises. Klein did not "shoot the messenger" when he got bad news promptly and his management team could take corrective action. Too many CEO's shoot the messenger and, as a result, potential problems are not promptly disclosed and addressed.

Following a decade long relationship, Klein also retained Chartwell to provide advice and help negotiate the acquisition of the bank by BB&T in 2002.

Small Community Banks

Over the years, Chartwell has advised numerous community banking clients across the country as the result of a bank encountering operational and/or regulatory problems. In most cases Chartwell was contacted by the bank's CEO or someone on the bank's board of directors at the suggestion of another banker or the bank's law firm.

Most of these assignments originated as a result of regulatory problems related to bad loans, operational deficiencies and/or inadequate management. Several of these assignments did result in the sale of the institution to a larger bank.

Early Internet: Venture Capital

In 1996, Chartwell took a detour into the early Internet and helped fund a small private California based company engaged in the development and deployment of a push-to-talk [PTT] radio system that was designed to utilize encrypted voice over the Internet [VOIP] to connect users. The system also utilized GPS to map the location of individual users.

This Internet based system was marketed to military and transportation users. Early prototype systems were installed by a friendly foreign military and in several domestic commercial applications. This technology was very unique twenty years ago. Today such features are common on numerous systems such as Vonage, Nextel [Sprint], the iPhone etc.

This technology was perhaps offered too early and the company never seemed to get it to work as advertised on a large-scale project. However, the major issue was management.

The company's founder and President made great presentations but he was slow on delivery. From a governance viewpoint he would tell you what you wanted to hear and then he proceeded to do something else. A classic entrepreneur, he simply ignored any external advice from investors.

Needless to say, a great idea with poor management does not represent a great investment and the investment in this early Internet based communications company was a complete loss.

Kentucky: Trans Financial Bank

In 1996, Trans Financial was a $2.0 billion multi-bank holding company based Bowling Green, Kentucky, home of the GM Corvette plant.

Trans Financial had grown rapidly, more than doubling in size through a series of community bank acquisitions in the early 1990's. In 1993, Trans Financial's CEO initiated a strategic decision to change this community banking organization into a diversified financial services provider.

The result three years later was a company burdened with a wide array of poorly performing nonbank operations. Three years of disappointing results culminated in action by the board of directors to replace the company's CEO.

Vince Berta, the company's CFO, was promoted to President & CEO in June 1996. Berta had joined Trans Financial as CFO from PNC Bank a few years earlier.

In Chapter Three I described how Beverly Taylor, the manager of my financial analysis team at Citizens Fidelity hired Berta as a new analyst in 1982. Taylor had excellent "people insight" and my philosophy was to give managers the authority to hire their own staff. Managers would sink or swim with their decisions and I only requested the opportunity to meet potential employees before they started work.

When Taylor asked me what I thought of Berta after our initial introduction I responded, "Are you sure?" She was and Berta was not only an outstanding analyst at Citizens - he succeeded me as head of the finance division following PNC's acquisition of the bank. His career eventually took him to PNC's headquarters in Pittsburgh. In 1993, Berta was enticed by an offer to become CFO of Trans Financial and moved to Bowling Green.

As CEO, Berta quickly shifted Trans Financial's focus back to its core banking franchise and the company exited its non-core businesses. The company's improved financial performance (ROE: 17%] attracted the interest of several potential aquirors in 1998. In response, Berta undertook an analysis of Trans Financial's strategic alternatives and sought advice from selected legal and investment firms, including Chartwell Capital.

Berta had extensive merger and acquisition experience and was well qualified to evaluate Trans Financial's strategic alternatives. He was my key resource as Citizens Fidelity acquired 10 banks in the 1980's and was at my side during our negotiations to be acquired by PNC.

Berta also wanted the best advice available and we engaged Ed Herlihy at Wachtell Lipton in New York to provide both legal and strategic advice.

The Trans Financial story ends with one of the highest acquisition premiums reported in the 1990's. The result was a transaction with Star Bank (now US Bank) at 4.6 times tangible book value. Berta did an excellent job as CEO at Trans Financial and the results are described in my book: "*It Is What It Is*".

Kentucky & California: Rusnak

My previous book, "*It Is What It Is*", also describes Chartwell's relationship with Pat Rusnak, an example of what I call a "second generation" relationship. In business, many people seem to want to develop their own new relationships with peers and do not seek out or try to retrain relationships with the associates of their previous managers.

Rusnak worked in the finance division of Trans Financial. Following the acquisition of Trans Financial in 1998, Rusnak had been recruited to join United Community Bank in Georgia as Controller. Berta recommended Rusnak contact me to assist with a strategic assessment of the bank's operations. This was the first of a series of projects with Rusnak.

In 2000, Rusnak accepted the CFO position at Humboldt Bancorp and moved his family from Georgia to Eureka on the northern coast of California.

It's always been Rusnak's practice to call me early in the morning – prior to 8:00 AM Eastern Time. I leave it to your imagination to calculate the impact of his morning calls from the west coast time zone to me on the east coast.

"Charles, this is Pat."

In 2001, Rusnak invited me to assist with his evaluation of Humboldt's operations and strategic alternatives. We included investment bankers from Keefe Bruyette & Woods [KBW] in the process to evaluate both the potential for acquisitions by Humboldt and Humboldt's acquisition by potential merger partners.

Following this careful analysis of the build versus sell alternatives and extensive board discussions, the board elected to remain independent and recruited a new CEO following the retirement of the current CEO.

The build strategy was successful and in 2004, three years after our initial analysis, Umpqua Holdings, a $5.0 billion bank holding company based in Portland, Oregon, acquired Humboldt Bancorp. This acquisition of Humboldt and its 27 locations was Umpqua's initial entry into California. Following the acquisition, Rusnak was asked to join Umpqua as EVP & CFO of the California Region.

In 2005, Western Sierra Bancorp, located in the Sacramento area, initiated a search for a Chief Operating Officer [COO] and, not surprisingly, identified an ideal candidate in their backyard. Rusnak was recruited to Western Sierra where he was responsible for management of the finance/accounting, compliance, internal audit, human resources, operations and information technology functions of this $1.3 billion multi-bank holding company.

Umpqua Holdings continued its expansion into California and acquired Western Sierra in 2006. The CEO of Humboldt Bancorp had moved to Spokane, Washington, as CEO of AmericanWest Bank following the acquisition of Humboldt by Umpqua. The acquisition of Western Sierra now provided him the opportunity to recruit Rusnak as COO of AmericanWest.

Financial Crisis & AmericanWest Bank

Rusnak probably didn't appreciate it at the time, but he was well prepared for his move to Spokane as COO of AmericanWest in September 2006. He had ten years experience in managing problems, divesting businesses, and improving operating efficiency combined with successful internal growth and growth by acquisition.

Few community bank finance and operating executives had the credit experience Rusnak had gained during the nation's ten-year boom economy that had concealed a growing mountain of real estate debt that would soon turn ugly. His abilities would soon be put to the test.

Asset quality problems began to surface in AmericanWest's Utah operations in mid 2007. The expansion into Utah, initiated by the CEO prior to Rusnak joining the bank as COO, was to become the "Achilles Heel" of AmericanWest.

No surprise that these credit problems were real estate related, and Rusnak initiated actions to address the problems being identified in the Utah portfolio. The bank ceased origination of new residential development loans in 2007 in recognition of the deteriorating market conditions. Rusnak also initiated a careful credit review of residential construction and development loans, resulting in a significant increase in the bank's provision for loan losses for the fourth quarter of 2007.

June 2008: US Senator Chuck Schumer [D-NY] wrote a letter to bank regulators questioning the viability of IndyMac Bank, one of the nation's largest home lenders based in Pasadena, California. The letter became public and started a two-week, $1.3 billion deposit run on IndyMac, culminating with national television coverage of long lines of depositors outside the IndyMac offices waiting to withdraw their money – the nation was witnessing a classic bank run for the first time since the 1930's.

July 2008: IndyMac was closed on a Friday and all of the insured deposit accounts were transferred to a new bridge bank owned by the FDIC. No buyer was located for IndyMac and deposits over $100,000 were not covered by FDIC insurance.

The Wall Street crisis had now come to Main Street and many banks, including AmericanWest, experienced significant deposit withdrawals.

July 2008: AmericanWest announced the resignation of the CEO at the request of the board of directors and Rusnak was appointed President and CEO. Time was of the essence and Rusnak does not waste time.

"Charles, this is Pat, I would like you to fly to Spokane."

I accepted Rusnak's invitation and Chartwell was retained as a financial advisor in early August to assist AmericanWest with liquidity and capital planning.

Before continuing, I think it's important to note that from July 2008 onward, Rusnak's focus was always forward, not backward. I never heard Rusnak in public or private criticize anyone for the decisions and actions that eventually led to the bank's increasingly dire circumstances.

Rusnak was always focused on what needed to be done to resolve problems, not looking for someone to blame. I believe his professional attitude helped create the positive, forward-looking attitude exhibited by his entire management team.

In early 2007, Chartwell had been retained by another bank located in the Midwest to conduct a Management Study as required by a regulatory order for that bank. This earlier project and other assignments combined with my selection as Chairman of the American Association of Bank Directors had provided me with unique insight into the approach of bank regulators and the management of operating issues faced by banks operating under regulatory orders.

AmericanWest's Support Center became the action central for management activity. It was months before I realized that Rusnak also had access to the prior CEO's large corner office in the bank's downtown headquarters. To my knowledge he never moved into that corner office – he was too busy and unpretentious.

Rusnak was completely focused on the job at hand and started working from his small office in the finance section of the Support Center. The Controller and Treasurer occupied the two larger corner offices on the floor just a few feet away. Based on the size of his office, any casual visitor would have mistaken Rusnak for a staff accountant – not the CEO.

It's probably best none of us had time to watch television. This is the first financial crisis covered hour-by-hour on national television. In my opinion, the all-day business coverage on CNBC and other news channels had a significant negative impact on public confidence – and deposit runs are created by a lack of confidence. The business and other news channels all appeared to be competing with one another to deliver the latest market rumor and self-fulfilling bad news.

The events of September 2008 have been covered in great detail by numerous articles and books, so this story will not cover unnecessary ground. The point is to illustrate the market conditions that were unfolding as Rusnak and his management team were restructuring the bank.

September 7, 2008: The Federal Housing Finance Agency [FHFA] placed Fannie Mae and Freddie Mac, two government-sponsored enterprises [GSEs] that play a critical role in the US home mortgage market, into conservatorship. As conservator, the FHFA had full power to control the assets and operations of the firms.

The US Treasury put in place a set of financing agreements to ensure that the GSEs continued to meet their obligations to holders of the bonds they issued or guaranteed. The US taxpayer now stood behind about $5 trillion of GSE debt. However, dividends for the GSE's common and preferred shareholders were suspended.

Government officials reported this step was taken because a default by either of the two institutions, which had been battered by the downturn in housing and credit markets, would have caused severe disruptions in global financial markets, made home mortgages more difficult and expensive to obtain, and produced negative repercussions throughout the nation's economy.

Fortunately, AmericanWest had a relatively small investment portfolio and, unlike many community banks, owned no GSE preferred stock. The decision to suspend dividends on the GSE preferred shares sent shockwaves through the capital markets – these shares had been considered safe "bank eligible" investments until the day the government decided to stop payment. Numerous community banks took a serious hit to their capital positions with no regulatory help in sight.

September 15, 2008: On Monday morning, one week later, Lehman Brothers filed for bankruptcy following a massive exodus of liquidity, loss of clients, a dramatic decline in stock value and the devaluation of its assets by the rating agencies the prior week.

Lehman, with $600 billion in assets, was the largest bankruptcy in US history. The market was well aware that Lehman was in trouble and was expecting some type of resolution, but not bankruptcy. The global impact was beyond comprehension. Allowing Lehman to descend to bankruptcy may have been the worst decision made during the entire financial crisis.

September 25, 2008: Lehman Brothers was followed ten days later by the seizure of Washington Mutual [WAMU] on a Thursday after the bank experienced the withdrawal of over $16 billion in deposits during what was described as a 10-day deposit run reflecting a significant loss of depositor confidence following the GSE and Lehman announcements.

Washington Mutual was the sixth largest bank in the nation with over $300 billion of deposits, and was the largest bank failure in American financial history. Fortunately, unlike IndyMac, the FDIC had a buyer this time, and JP Morgan reopened the bank the next day as JP Morgan Chase offices.

September 29, 2008: On Monday morning the FDIC announced that following weekend negotiations, Citibank was acquiring Wachovia in an "open bank" transaction with financial support provided by the FDIC.

Market reaction was confused, and the confusion was further compounded when the FDIC permitted Wells Fargo to propose another approach to the transaction within days. Ultimately, after a public legal battle, Wells Fargo acquired Wachovia. The FDIC's actions and the uncertain outcome of the transaction further unsettled the financial markets.

Wachovia, the nation's fourth largest bank with $800 billion of assets, suffered a significant stock decline and reported deposit withdrawals of $5.0 billion following the failure of Washington Mutual. Wachovia's credit problems were related to its 2006 acquisition of Golden West, the second largest savings & loan in the nation. Golden West had specialized in option ARM loans marketed under the name "Pick-A-Pay," a product now considered toxic by the credit markets.

In just one short month, the nation had witnessed the government takeover of two government sponsored mortgage institutions [including the taxpayer guarantee of $5 trillion in GSE debt], the largest bankruptcy in the nation's history with Lehman Brothers, the largest bank failure in the nation's history at Washington Mutual, and the near failure of Wachovia, the nation's fourth largest bank.

These external problems were producing terrible headlines at a time when AmericanWest was facing its own internal challenges, including building liquidity, undertaking major organizational changes, identifying more problem loans, making preparations to report another significant quarterly loss, and attempting to raise new capital.

This was definitely not a good environment for AmericanWest to report more bad news!

AmericanWest had retained Sandler O'Neil, a New York based investment-banking firm, to raise new capital for the bank. Over the coming months, Al Glowasky and his associates at Sandler would work the phones, arrange meetings, sign non-disclosure agreements, arrange due diligence and successfully negotiate several term sheets. Glowasky's "never say die" approach was an essential ingredient in the recipe that saved the bank.

A wide variety of investors were involved in these discussions. They ranged from hedge funds that sent very inexperienced MBAs who didn't have a clue about analyzing a troubled bank to very experienced investors that had participated in bank recapitalizations in the early 1990's.

The most frustrating meetings were with potential investors that had a blend of experience, as it was nearly impossible for us to determine if they really knew what they were doing in a very uncertain economic and investment environment.

"Big Hat – No Cattle"

In the Midwest and we have a saying about want-to-be cowboys – they always looked the part [Big Hat] but owned no cattle. Many of the potential investors talked a good story [Big Hat] but most lacked the financial experience and capacity [No Cattle] to complete a transaction.

It was becoming abundantly clear that potential investors were not willing to invest in the holding company if it required full repayment of the almost $50 million of Trust Preferred Securities [TruPS] outstanding at the holding company. On the other hand, if recapitalization took place at the bank level it was obvious that the holding company would need to declare bankruptcy. This was a daunting thought.

Chartwell prepared a memo for discussion with the board of directors that outlined an approach to recapitalize the bank rather than the holding company. Bankruptcy for the holding company would be a tough alternative for board members to consider.

Bankruptcy would render the holding company's outstanding shares worthless. The latest proxy reported that board members and executive management owned over 600,000 shares that in late 2007 had represented over $12 million in value. Those shares would now be worthless with no chance of recovery.

As a practical matter, the company's shares were already essentially worthless with no chance to return to previous levels. The shares were trading at less than $0.25 per share and had been delisted by NASDAQ on March 4, 2010 – shareholder value had declined by over $350 million during the past two years and the total shareholder value was now less than $5 million. The value of AWBC shares was already nominal and would be completely worthless if the bank were to be seized by bank regulators.

June 2010: The board signed on to our bankruptcy strategy after considerable debate and discussion with the bank's legal and financial advisors. Glowasky had his marching orders and Jay Simmons, AmericanWest's General Counsel, initiated steps to start the process.

Simmons joined Rusnak at AmericanWest in April 2008. Prior to accepting the position at AmericanWest he had been Vice President and Legal Counsel for Zions Bank, a position he had accepted after the acquisition of Trans Financial in Kentucky where he and Rusnak had worked together in the 1990's.

Simmons and Rusnak selected Morrison & Foerster [MoFo] in San Francisco and Henry Fields, a Partner at MoFo, as the lead attorney for the proposed transaction. Fields had worked with Rusnak and myself in 2001 to help liquidate the leasing subsidiary at Humboldt Bank.

Glowasky had identified SKBHC Holdings as a potential acquiror of AmericanWest Bank. However, SKBHC still required approval as a bank holding company by the Federal Reserve.

October 2010: The Federal Reserve Board announced its approval of the proposal by SKBHC Holdings LLC, Corona del Mar, California, to become a bank holding company. SKBHC was now in a position to move forward with the AmericanWest transaction.

This announcement allowed the AmericanWest holding company to execute the definitive agreement with SKBHC, for the sale of the bank as part of the company's soon-to-be-filed Chapter 11 bankruptcy.

December 2, 2010: The Federal Reserve approved the acquisition of AmericanWest Bank by SKBHC Holdings. Another significant step was completed.

December 9, 2010: The bankruptcy court approved the purchase of the bank by SKBHC from AmericanWest Bancorporation. SKBHC could now move forward with plans to acquire and invest up to $200 million to recapitalize the bank.

December 20th marked the beginning of a new chapter for AmericanWest Bank as a "well-capitalized" financially strong institution. The board and Rusnak had achieved their final goal of saving the bank from seizure by the FDIC and protecting the jobs of over 500 employees at AmericanWest.

Rusnak was presented with an a heartfelt, leather bound "In Gratitude" book consisting of family photographs and personal "Thank You" messages from the employees at every bank location for his dedication and leadership. I was grateful to be included at this employee meeting - words cannot describe the emotion and appreciation displayed by all in attendance at that "Thank You" tribute.

SKBHC had their own executive management team and following the "Thank You" tribute Rusnak handed the keys to the bank to the new management team - he then drove home to enjoy the Christmas holidays with his family.

Rusnak is currently CFO of a $21 billion asset bank in California.

Financial Crisis: Management Studies

Chartwell also conducted a number of "Management Studies" required by bank regulators for troubled banks during the financial crisis. Many bank directors were surprised to discover that bank regulators could require their board to retain an independent firm to conduct an analysis that could then make recommendations to their board for board and management changes at their institution.

Bank boards were required to submit the name of the firm they wanted to select to bank regulators for approval. Bank regulators approved Chartwell to conduct a number of such Management Studies during the financial crisis.

A typical regulatory order would require a Management Study to address the following:

1. Identify the type and number of officer positions needed to properly manage and supervise the affairs of the bank;

2. Identify and establish board and management committees as are needed to provide guidance and oversight to active management;

3. Evaluate executive officers, senior lending officers and credit staff to determine whether these individuals possess the ability, experience and other qualifications required to perform present and anticipated duties;

4. Evaluate board members, executive officers and senior lending staff; including an evaluation of compensation, including salaries, incentive plans, director fees, and other benefits; and

5. Develop a plan to replace, recruit and hire any additional or replacement personnel with the requisite ability,

experience and other qualifications to fill those officer or staff member positions identified as deficient.

6. Within 30 days after receipt of the Management Study, the board was required to formulate a "Plan" to implement the recommendations of the Management Study.

7. The Plan was submitted to and subject to approval by the bank's regulators.

Chartwell's first study was for a bank in Lexington, Kentucky. This bank had grown rapidly and had recently expanded into a new market by acquisition. The bank's most recent regulatory exam had uncovered significant operational and credit problems.

The bank's regulators required the board to retain a firm to perform a Management Study and the bank's outside law firm suggested the board's Chairman contact Chartwell.

In response to the operational problems, the bank hired Denise Van Steenlandt as its new Chief Operating Officer [COO] at the same time Chartwell was retained to conduct the Management Study. Van Steenlandt proved to be an outstanding executive and she became the "go to" person for accurate information. Following completion of Chartwell's assessment, the board replaced the bank's CEO, Chief Loan Officer and CFO.

Bank regulators had also been critical of the bank's Chief Credit Officer [CCO] due to the bank's serious credit problems. However, Chartwell determined that this individual was well qualified and the bank's CEO and Chief Loan Officer had circumvented his credit authority and ignored his credit opinions. The bank's regulators accepted Chartwell's conclusion and this individual remained with the new management team.

Chartwell worked with the bank's new CEO and board for several subsequent years as the bank executed its plan to resolve operational problems, reduce problem credits and downsize with the sale of branches.

Van Steenlandt successfully resolved the bank's operational problems, recruited new managers for key operations and helped downsize the bank. Once she finished these tasks her job was completed and she resigned.

Van Steenlandt had earned my respect and I asked her to work with me at Chartwell on a number of future Management Studies.

Van Steenlandt has a unique ability to interview and accurately assess the potential capability of individual bank directors, officers and staff. Time proved her judgment and opinion was frequently more accurate than mine. Van Steenlandt is another prime example of how I have benefited from the talents of other people.

Our first Management Study together was for another community bank that had encountered credit problems and received a regulatory order. Each future assignment was different but our approach was similar.

Our first step was a series of interviews with board members and executive officers. We did not take notes during these "visits" as I have found people are not candid when you take notes during an interview. We found that once people relaxed during our visits they would become very candid with their comments.

"You can observe a lot by just watching"
Yogi Berra

At one institution we found the credit approval process looked good on paper but, in fact, did not work. When we attended a credit meeting in process it was clear the officers were taking no responsibility for analyzing credit and recommending loans. The lending officers and credit staff would present a new loan to the board's loan committee consisting of three board members and then ask, "What do you think?"

When we asked the bank's officers about individual problem loans the standard answer was always, "the board approved the loan". We could find no lending officer, credit officer or bank executive that would take any personal responsibility for a problem loan.

We described this process as "delegating up" to the board. The board members had indicated to us that they had wanted to control the credit approval process but, as they had no credit experience, the entire process was ineffective.

Our final report recommended replacing the CEO and the credit approval process was reorganized to assign responsibility for credit approval to bank management with board oversight.

This Management Study certainly supported the position of the American Association of Bank Directors [AABD] that bank directors should not approve loans. Credit approval is a complex process and requires time, training and experience; attributes not shared by most bank directors.

In my opinion, if board members do not have confidence in their bank's management then they need to replace management, not try to solve the problem by "stepping into management's shoes". Even directors with prior credit experience should not insert themselves into day-to-day management; a board member's job is oversight.

Another Management Study uncovered a credit approval and incentive compensation conflict that contributed to credit problems related to the bank's expansion into a new market. In this case we discovered the board had designated a Chief Credit Officer [CCO] in response to a previous regulatory criticism. On the surface, the bank had complied with the previous regulatory request to create an independent credit approval function.

However, the interview process told a different story. The CCO was still actively involved in the origination of new loans in the bank's new market. These new loans were assigned to other officers but were, in fact, credit relationships of the CCO.

"You get what you pay for"

To complicate matters, when this individual was elected CCO his incentive compensation plan was not changed and his annual bonus was linked to loan growth rather than credit quality. My experience indicates that you get what you pay for and as a result the bank accumulated poor quality loans in its new market.

We also discovered strong "we" verses "they" conflict between the staff in the home community and the new market. We frequently discovered a lack of common purpose and teamwork in these troubled banks.

Our Management Studies required careful analysis and consideration as our conclusions and recommendations would have serious consequences on the careers of people at the bank. At one institution we encountered "social media" retaliation as anonymous and slanderous comments were posted about Van Steenlandt on a local news website.

On another occasion, the bank, Chartwell, Van Steenlandt and myself were all subject to litigation by a bank officer we had recommended be replaced. In this case, the issue was really created by the FDIC refusing to let the bank pay the officer a relatively small amount due under his employment contract.

The final result was that the bank spent several times the original amount in question on legal fees before the legal action against the bank, Chartwell, Van Steenlandt and myself was dismissed and the FDIC finally approved a financial settlement with the officer.

In 2013, the board of a troubled bank recruited Van Steenlandt as CEO to address the bank's operational, personnel and credit problems. Once again she proved her ability to provide effective leadership and she stabilized the bank sufficiently for it to be considered a desirable market entry. The board of directors retained Chartwell to approach potential acquirors and a larger institution acquired the bank in late 2015.

Mergers & Acquisitions

During the past twenty-six years, Chartwell has been active as a financial advisor for bank acquisitions [M&A]. For example, based on announced M&A deal values Chartwell was nationally ranked #19 [$735 million] in 1998, #17 [$372 million] in 2001 and #33 [$109 million] in 2015 for whole bank acquisitions.

Chartwell has also been active in the purchase and sale of bank branch locations for clients and was ranked #5 nationwide in 2008 and #4 nationwide in 2009 for the number of branch transactions completed.

In 2008, I was surprised when the American Banker newspaper reported Chartwell was tied with Sandler O'Neil, the New York based investment firm, for the rank of #1 for the number of branch transactions in the first quarter.

To say the least, the market for branch transactions was distressed during the financial crisis and both firms had completed just two transactions during the first quarter of 2008. This limited activity had placed both firms in a nationwide tie for most branch transactions!

During my career I have been actively engaged in over $6.8 billion of financial transactions for financial institutions, corporations and institutional investors.

Kentucky: Hostile Takeover Defense

Bowling Green, KY, October 16, 2009 [PR Newswire]—Citizens First Corporation expressed surprise today that Porter Bancorp Inc. [NASDAQ: PBIB] announced that it had acquired Options to Purchase 15.8% of the Common Shares of Citizens First Corporation [NASDAQ: CZFC].

Citizens First wants to assure shareholders that it was not involved in this action and first learned of it in Porter Bancorp's press release. "We can only view this announcement as a hostile action by Porter Bancorp", commented Jack Sheidler, Citizens First Chairman.

October 23, 2009: Letter from Porter to Citizens First

The undersigned, Porter Bancorp, is offering $9.00 per share to all holders of common stock of Citizens First Corporation in exchange for each share of CZFC common stock tendered by the holder thereof [the "Exchange Offer"].

At the time of this offer, Citizens shares were trading at about $4.50 per share so an offer of $9.00 per share represented a potential 100% market premium.

Citizens First had been a Chartwell client for several years and we were immediately contacted by management and the board to provide advice. Citizens' largest shareholder was an investment fund affiliated with Commerce Street Capital in Texas. Obviously, our first call was to determine the interest of the bank's largest shareholder.

Chartwell's analysis of the situation indicated several issues with the proposal by Porter:

First, we questioned the value of the offer based on Porter's then stock price of about $16.00 per share. Our analysis indicated that the current price did not reflect the credit risks we suspected existed with their business model. However, the nature of their unfriendly proposal limited our ability to conduct due diligence.

Second, Porter's offer included a significant cash component and both banks were participants in the TARP program. Our analysis indicated that any cash component for an acquisition would violate the terms of the TARP agreement with US Treasury Department. Therefore, any acquisition by Porter would be restricted to an exchange of shares.

Representatives from Commerce Street reviewed Chartwell's analysis and prepared a detailed valuation for the Citizens board of directors that supported our conclusions.

Both firms presented our findings to the Citizens First board of directors and, following detailed discussions, the board elected to reject the offer by Porter. The board's rejection of the offer led to about six weeks of legal and regulatory maneuvering coordinated by Cindy Young and Caryn Price at Wyatt, Tarrant & Combs; the law firm representing Citizens. Young and Price led the law firm's banking practice following Stewart Conner's retirement. I should note that Young has worked with Chartwell on a number of assignments over the past twenty years.

Porter Bancorp Withdraws Exchange Offer:

LOUISVILLE, Ky., Dec 14, 2009 (BUSINESS WIRE) -- Porter Bancorp, Inc. (NASDAQ: PBIB) announced today that it has withdrawn its exchange offer to acquire all of the outstanding common shares of Citizens First Corporation (NASDAQ: CZFC) for $9.00 per share. The tender offer had been set to expire at 5:00 P.M. ET, on December 22, 2009.

"Porter Bancorp has elected to withdraw its tender offer to acquire Citizens First of Bowling Green due to our inability to fully evaluate the Citizens First transaction," stated Maria L. Bouvette, Porter Bancorp's President and Chief Executive Officer. "The distraction of proceeding on a hostile basis, continued softness in the economy and real estate markets, the current regulatory environment for financial institutions, and the lack of cooperation

from Citizens First's board and management created an unacceptable level of uncertainty for us in this transaction. As a result, we will not pursue the exchange offer at this time and will remain focused on managing Porter's core operations in our existing markets."

Over the next two years, Porter disclosed an increasing level of non-performing assets. Porter's stock price experienced a significant decline from $16.00 per share to under $1.00 per share; as a result, Porter's proposed exchange offer represented less than $1.00 per share for Citizens First.

Date	Citizens Price	Porter Price	Exchange Ratio	Exchange Value
10/2009	$4.50	$16.00	.5686	$9.10
2/2010	$6.80	$10.96	.5686	$6.23
11/2012	$8.15	$0.90	.5686	$0.58
5/2016	$14.12	$1.75	.5686	$1.00

Whereas, as illustrated above, Citizens stock price increased during this same period of time.

It's not often the stock market provides a clear post-decision result that vindicates a board's rejection of an exchange offer that might initially appear to offer a 100% premium to a firm's current stock price.

Jack Sheidler, independent board Chairman, and Todd Kanipe, President & CEO, guided the board of directors of Citizens First through a challenging decision process. Subsequent events validated that the board made the right decision at the right time.

East Coast: ATM Fraud

This last story is just an unusual event that is being shared to illustrate the diversity of issues that involved Chartwell.

A dozen years ago, a client had acquired a bank that serviced a geographically diverse group of private ATMs located in stores. The bank decided this was a business risk they did not want to retain and made plans to exit the business.

On the last day of the exit strategy the individual servicing the ATMs in a distant state disappeared with several hundred thousand dollars of cash that was supposed to be in the ATMs.

I received a call several weeks after the event reporting that this individual had been found dead in his van under mysterious circumstances near Fort Lauderdale.

The police had impounded the van with several unopened boxes but would not give the bank access. The client was asking Chartwell for some local contacts. My first suggestion was to hire a private firm to watch the van – what if those unguarded boxes contained the cash? However, no cash was discovered when the bank obtained entry to the van.

The bank's private investigation determined the thief had made a new friend in Florida and they had a joint safety deposit box – that did in fact contain part but not all of the cash.

Further investigation determined that the thief and his new friend had frequented a neighborhood drug house. A search of the drug house revealed several unopened boxes in a back room that contained several hundred thousand dollars of cash!

With this discovery the bank had recovered most of the money. Truth is stranger than fiction; drug addicts had unknowingly been sitting on the boxes that contained the money!

Future Activity?

Chartwell continues to be actively working with mostly second and third generation clients. At present, we are working on a couple of potential acquisition assignments, a strategic planning assignment and as an expert witness in a securities case. The diversity of these challenges and the ability to be associated with quality people is what keeps work interesting.

This book does not represent the final chapter for Chartwell's activities.

"It ain't over till it's over"

Yogi Berra

Chapter Six

Keefe Partners

Harry V Keefe [1922-2002] was the founder [1962], Chairman and Chief Executive Officer [CEO] of Keefe, Bruyette & Woods, [KBW] a New York investment firm specializing in commercial banks. He resigned from KBW in 1989 to organize Keefe Managers to serve as the investment advisor for Keefe Partners, an investment partnership [hedge fund] for bank and thrift securities.

Keefe and I had been acquainted for about fifteen years; however, I certainly would not have described us as friends. I was somewhat surprised when Keefe contacted me about investing and working in some capacity with Keefe Partners.

We discussed several possible arrangements and we agreed that an arrangement with Chartwell Capital would be a workable relationship. I invested in the fund, Keefe appointed me to the funds board of advisors and Chartwell was engaged from time to time to perform investment due diligence.

This relationship with Keefe and Keefe Partners clearly helped give Chartwell Capital a kick-start and credibility with potential clients. It also helped expand my relationships with both bankers and investors.

The financial markets were just starting to recover from what has been described as the Savings & Loan Crisis. The FDIC reported 1,400 bank and thrift failures between 1989 and 1993 and the crisis produced thousands of troubled thrifts and banks across the country.

This financial climate set the stage for Keefe Partners to selectively participate in the recapitalization of troubled financial institutions. Over the years Chartwell performed due-diligence on dozens of such investments for Keefe Partners.

Keefe, known for using a very large slide rule to compute ratios, was a remarkable individual with a deep knowledge of banks and financial markets. I always enjoyed discussing individual banks and potential investments with him. Without question, I learned an enormous amount about bank investing from Keefe.

Keefe also wanted to surround himself with the best people he could identify. One such person was Matt Byrnes, a young banker that Keefe recruited to join the fund's analytical team. A bank officer at a New York bank had described Byrnes as an outstanding individual and Keefe invited Byrnes to an evening visit at Keefe Partners. At the conclusion of that visit Keefe invited Byrnes to join Keefe Partners.

When Byrnes returned home that evening he told his wife, Hélène, he was going to accept Keefe's offer. When she asked, "What will he pay you?" the answer was "He didn't say". That decision by Byrnes speaks to Keefe's reputation and it certainly turned out to be a great decision by Byrnes.

Byrnes and I worked together on a wide variety of assignments for Keefe and Byrnes proved to be an outstanding analyst and investor. My records indicate that we worked on investments across the country; including California, Missouri, Louisiana, Texas, Arizona, Ohio, New Jersey, Florida, etc.

Some investments were more work than others and the Arizona investment certainly comes to mind. Federal anti-trust law required Bank of America to sell certain Arizona branches following its acquisition of Security Pacific Bank in 1992.

The Arizona branch locations and associated deposits and loans were consolidated into a new bank charter to be capitalized by private investors. Arizona was a growing market and the prospects for this existing bank franchise certainly looked promising.

Following due diligence, Keefe Partners invested in the new bank and Chartwell helped identify other investors to complete the capitalization.

However, the spike in interest rates that occurred in 1994 had an unexpected negative impact on the value of the bank's investment portfolio. The bank's asset/liability computer program did not accurately forecast potential market values.

Many bank investment professionals will state that portfolio yield is more important than market value as bank regulators don't include market value adjustments in regulatory capital. Bank regulators may not calculate market value as part of regulatory capital but they clearly pay close attention.

In the case of this Arizona bank the regulators required the investors to add capital or sell the bank. The investors were certainly disappointed in management's performance. Rather than invest more capital, a decision was made to engage an investment banker to sell the bank. Fortunately, the Arizona market was considered to be attractive and the bank was sold at a modest profit for the investors.

The original plan had been to recruit new management to the bank at the time the new capitalization occurred but the board of directors was slow to act. Another lesson learned about the importance of having the right team in place day one.

As time progressed Keefe entrusted Byrnes with more day-to-day portfolio management. The compound annual return of my investment account with Keefe Partners was over 20% for the 12 years between 1990 and 2002. My only regret was not investing more money with Keefe Partners.

Keefe had recruited a first class team at Keefe Partners and the results, once again, demonstrate the importance of consistently working with the best people you can identify.

In 1998, Chartwell conducted due-diligence for Keefe Partners on a potential investment in Republic Bank in St Petersburg, Florida. Keefe decided to make a significant investment in the bank's recapitalization and I was asked to join the bank's board of directors. The Republic story is described in Chapter Ten.

Keefe also introduced me to Ed Herlihy, the banking partner at Wachtell Lipton in New York. Herlihy has been one of the leading bank attorneys for several decades and has been a consistent and valued advisor for years. Herlihy served as the attorney for both the Trans Financial and Republic Bank acquisitions. But most important, Herlihy has always promptly retuned my phone calls – very impressive for such a busy professional.

Herlihy is another example of the importance of identifying the best resources available and my thanks go to him for the advice he has provided to me over the past twenty years.

Keefe became a close friend and for many years Molly and I enjoyed spending the New Year's holiday aboard our boats with Harry and, his wife, Anita, in Palm Beach. I learned a great deal from Keefe and missed his sage advice during the 2007-2009 financial crises as he had passed away in 2002. Molly and I have remained friends with Anita and we continue to enjoy periodic visits together.

Byrnes departed Keefe Partners in 1999 to start his own hedge fund, SuNova Capital, to invest in financial institutions. Having established strong relationships with both Keefe and Byrnes I decided to invest with both firms.

Byrnes gets credit for not "gating" [restricting] SuNova withdrawals when the financial crisis hit in 2008 and he decided to return money to his investors and close the fund. SuNova still produced an enviable record with my account achieving a 17% annualized return over the eight-year period of my investment in his hedge fund.

Byrnes and I have now known one another for twenty-five years. He remains a close personal friend, we enjoy family visits and I continue to value his advice. This is another example of how working with quality people leads to working with even more quality people.

Chapter Seven

Sunbeam Corporation

In 1990, Sunbeam Corporation acquired the business of Allegheny International, Pittsburgh, Pennsylvania; pursuant to a court-approved plan of bankruptcy reorganization. Japonica Partners was the plan sponsor and Steinhardt Partners [a New York based hedge fund] and Mutual Series Fund [publically traded mutual fund] formed the investor group that provided the equity financing.

Chartwell Capital was retained by the investment group to help negotiate a settlement with Allegheny's bank lenders who were opposed to the investment group's hostile acquisition of Allegheny. A settlement was achieved and the court approved the acquisition. Allegheny was renamed Sunbeam-Oster Company [later shortened to Sunbeam] and operated as a private company following the bankruptcy reorganization.

Following the acquisition, I was elected to the board of directors of Sunbeam pursuant to the court-approved plan, and served as a member of the Executive Committee and as Chairman of the Audit Committee. Roderick Hills, [1931 – 2014] former Counselor to President Ford and former Chairman of the Securities & Exchange Commission, was also a new member of Sunbeam's board and this began a 20+ year personal relationship with Hills.

Sunbeam's headquarters were initially moved from Pittsburgh to Providence, Rhode Island. Sunbeam reemerged as a public company in 1992 when Sunbeam was listed on the New York Stock Exchange following the issuance of common stock to public shareholders. Steinhardt Partners and Mutual Series retained an 80% ownership interest following this initial public offering.

In January 1993, the board of directors terminated Sunbeam's Chairman & Chief Executive Officer [CEO] and elected me as interim Chairman and CEO. The CEO's termination resulted in significant media coverage. In addition to serving as Chairman, I served as the sole contact for both the press and the investment community during this period and accumulated a thick notebook of press coverage by the Wall Street Journal and New York Times.

One morning prior to a board meeting in New York City the newspapers reported that the former CEO had initiated litigation claiming damages of $2.0 billion for wrongful termination. I recall receiving a call from a reporter at the New York Times early that morning asking for a reaction. My response was "I haven't seen the complaint so therefore I have no comment". He then asked how it felt to be personally sued for $2.0 billion and I responded; [off the record] "I'm flattered".

"I will look after the goose, while you fight over the eggs."

In fact, the litigation only involved the investment group, not the company nor me. My approach became "I will look after the goose while you guys fight over the eggs". However, it was clearly in the best interest of the company that this very public dispute be resolved.

As this litigation initiated by the former CEO unfolded we determined that it was also necessary for Sunbeam to replace its Chief Financial Officer [CFO] and General Counsel due to certain potential conflicts and allegations that documents pertaining to the litigation had not been preserved.

Seriously in need of an in-house legal counsel, I contacted Stewart Conner, Managing Partner of the Wyatt, Tarrant & Combs law firm in Louisville for advice. My plan was to retain an individual from an outside law firm to act as a full-time in-house legal counsel to address the growing multitude of legal issues.

I visited Conner in Louisville and he recommended David Fannin, a partner at the firm's office in Louisville. Fannin had been in practice for twenty years with his focus on corporate law. Fannin returned to Rhode Island with me the next day and that started my 20+ year relationship with Fannin.

At Sunbeam we faced a number of serious legal issues related to the termination and stock ownership position of the previous CEO. Fannin negotiated with several New York law firms to successfully resolve the stock ownership position and related litigation involving the investment group. This was a major accomplishment and provided the opportunity to recruit a new Chairman & CEO.

During this same period the executive in charge of Sunbeam's international operations suffered a health issue and I was in need of a replacement. We were extremely fortunate to recruit Paul Van Orden, a retired senior executive from General Electric to serve as interim head of international. Van Orden, a very experienced executive, was an invaluable resource to me in many ways and he joined Sunbeam's board of directors following the recruitment of the new CEO.

Several visits with operating management reminded me of my discussions with the CEO of Xerox in the 1970's about the challenge of changing a corporate culture. Most of operating management viewed Sunbeam as a "manufacturing company" – the company made products. They did not understand the value of a "consumer brand" and no consumer research was done.

In the minds of most operating management, their customers were Walmart, K Mart or department stores – their design, sales and marketing focus did not extend to the final consumer. This narrow focus and the mindset to manufacture domestically would become the company's "Achilles Heal" in 1996.

Operating efficiency was also not a universal goal. I witnessed a very busy outdoor gas grill facility during a visit with operating management. Management was very proud of how busy the plant appeared to be – what I witnessed was complete confusion. The plant had no organized production line, inefficient delivery of parts and a disorganized storage area for final product that resulted in damaged packaging for outdoor gas grills.

Cost accounting was also not a universal goal. During another visit I witnessed a very well organized manufacturing line at the Oster hair clipper facility. However, I just got a blank look when I asked what it cost to make a clipper.

On another occasion, I was reviewing plans for a new facility that would add substantially to fixed cost. The operating manager had all the cost detail but I received another blank look when I asked what amount of additional sales would be required to cover the new fixed cost and produce a profit. I obviously requested additional financial projections.

In my view, Sunbeam needed to recruit an experienced consumer products executive as its next CEO and reorganize the finance function with an experienced CFO to monitor costs, measure operating efficiency and focus on profitability.

Even with these challenges, Sunbeam completed several acquisitions and achieved solid operating results during my tour of duty in 1993. I was certainly pleased when Merrill Lynch reported that Sunbeam was the best performing stock in the household products industry during my term as Chairman & CEO.

In August 1993, Sunbeam recruited a veteran consumer products executive who had previously managed GE's worldwide appliance business as its new Chairman & CEO. I continued as Vice Chairman of the company until year-end 1993 with responsibility for corporate operations and the company's relocation to Fort Lauderdale, Florida. In this role I also assisted the new CEO with the recruitment of a new management team; including a CFO, General Counsel and Human Resources Executive.

Fannin was offered and accepted the position of General Counsel and he and his family moved to Fort Lauderdale, the location of Sunbeam's new corporate headquarters. I continued as a member of Sunbeam's board of directors following my resignation as interim Chairman and CEO.

During 1994 and 1995 Sunbeam's new management team expanded operations with a series of product acquisitions and the construction of a major new domestic manufacturing facility, which was intended to consolidate most domestic manufacturing.

However, domestic manufacturing was not successfully consolidated at the new facility, as offshore sourcing from China was more cost effective than even a new state-of-the-art domestic facility. The cost savings projected did not materialize and costs at Sunbeam began accelerating faster than sales and earnings suffered as a result.

Following these disappointing results Sunbeam's board of directors elected me as Vice Chairman in April 1996. Once again I assumed responsibility for corporate management and became the primary contact for the press and the investment community.

My first public test came on April 25, when I announced that [a] earnings estimates for the balance of 1996 were too high, [b] that the company was conducting an intensive review of its cost structure and [c] the board of directors had initiated a search for a new Chairman & CEO. I was pleased that the market demonstrated confidence in our actions, as the stock price remained essentially unchanged following my announcements.

During the executive search for Sunbeam's new Chairman & CEO it became apparent that my role in replacing both previous CEO's was a concern for candidates. I indicated to the executive search firm that I would plan to step down from the board a short time after a new CEO was hired if my remaining on the board was an impediment to hiring a new CEO.

In July 1996, Sunbeam elected "Chainsaw" Al Dunlap as its new Chairman & CEO. At that time Dunlap was a "celebrity CEO" who was a well-known turnaround executive. Dunlap began a massive restructuring of Sunbeam, replacing most of senior management and adding several new members to the board of directors.

Although he had presided over some earlier highly successful turnaround stories, Dunlap turned out to be a terrible choice and I cannot escape responsibility for his selection. Dunlap's previous experience had been "fixing" and then "selling" a company, not "fixing" and "owning".

During my lengthy pre-employment interview with Dunlap at his home we discussed the consolidating nature of the small appliance business. Sunbeam had grown over the years by acquiring a number of small single product companies that made bathroom scales, electric blankets, etc. The small appliance business was a consolidating industry and Sunbeam was one of several consolidators.

The board of directors had previously considered potential buyers for Sunbeam. However, we discovered there were no significant potential buyers for a company like Sunbeam. Based on our conversation, I was under the mistaken impression that Dunlap understood fixing Sunbeam would need to be a "fix" and "own" project, not a "fix" and "sell" strategy.

Consistent with the commitment I made during the executive search process, I resigned from Sunbeam's board of directors in April 1997.

The following events that took place after my resignation from Sunbeam's board of directors are described in more detail in the 1999 book *"Chainsaw"*, written by John A Byrne, then a senior writer for Business Week magazine.

Dunlap had written a book on his previous turnarounds and at Sunbeam he simply followed the strategies he described in his book. By the end of 1997 Dunlap announced he had completed the turnaround and he was anticipating the sale of the company consistent with his previous turnarounds; however, no buyer emerged.

As a result, in early 1998, Dunlap did a "turn around" of his own and announced plans to grow through major M&A activity. Sunbeam proceeded to borrow $2.0 billion from a group of banks and, in March 1998, announced the acquisition of The Coleman Company (a major manufacturer of outdoor and camping equipment), and two other small appliance companies, Mr. Coffee and First Alert.

A few months later an internal investigation initiated by the board and conducted by Fannin, who Dunlap had retained as General Counsel, uncovered significant accounting irregularities relating to certain transactions that occurred at year-end 1997 and early 1998.

In June 1998, the board of directors terminated Dunlap as Chairman & CEO of Sunbeam along with Sunbeam's CFO, who had been previously associated with Dunlap. This action was inevitably followed by an investigation by the Securities & Exchange Commission and a number of civil lawsuits were filed that named Sunbeam, Dunlap and others in the management team as defendants.

Sunbeam's financial condition continued to suffer from the scandal and the company passed through bankruptcy in 2002.

To Dunlap's regret, Fannin was an excellent General Counsel and demonstrated that his integrity could not be compromised. A top-flight executive, Fannin was recruited by Office Depot to serve as its new Executive Vice President & General Counsel. Although he is now retired, Fannin has remained a friend for 20+ years and I continue to respect his advice.

Following his interviews with me, Byrne described me in his book, "*Chainsaw*", as "Sunbeam's most knowledgeable director". This was certainly a nice compliment but this Sunbeam chapter is a prime example of my "scar tissue". During presentations I frequently get asked questions about my role at Sunbeam and audiences always appear surprised when I respond, "I cannot avoid responsibility, I hired "Chainsaw" Al Dunlap."

Too few people appear willing to acknowledge mistakes – and this was a colossal mistake. I certainly learned not to rely on press reports about a celebrity CEO who was only to eager to self-promote his prior accomplishments. In our interview Dunlap told me what I wanted to hear, however, he apparently did not appreciate that the lack of buyers for Sunbeam at that time prevented his "fix" and "sell" strategy.

One final note, Sunbeam emerged from bankruptcy in 2002 and in 2005 was acquired by Jarden Corporation, a successful acquiror of consumer products companies. Jarden had grown to sufficient size to acquire Sunbeam eight years after Dunlap's ill-fated attempt to sell the company in 1997.

Jarden's products now include, Sunbeam, Oster, Mr. Coffee, First Alert and over a dozen other well-known consumer product brands. Jarden itself was acquired by Newell-Rubbermaid in 2016 to form Newell Brands. The consumer products industry has continued to consolidate as we expected but, following the 2002 bankruptcy, Sunbeam was no longer an acquiror.

Chapter Eight

Metro Bank

Louisville Development Bancorp [LDB], Louisville, Kentucky, was organized in 1996 as the holding company for a new bank, now named Metro Bank. LDB's shareholders include Kentucky's major banks and corporations and Metro Bank is dedicated to job creation and home ownership in the Louisville metro area. LDB is a shareholder-owned, for-profit, holding company for Metro Bank, a FDIC-insured commercial bank.

Several people, including the Mayor and Stewart Conner at the Wyatt law firm, asked if I would consider joining LDB's board of directors. They suggested that as Louisville had been good to me it would be good for me to "give back" some of my time and experience to Louisville. I accepted their invitation and served as an unpaid advisory board member for sixteen years, from 1997 until 2013. To be fair, I was reimbursed for travel expenses.

> *"We make a living by what we get,*
> *we make a life by what we give."*
> **Sir Winston Churchill**

Metro Bank opened its doors in January 1997 with $8.0 million in equity financing and $20 million in pledged deposits. This tiny banking organization opened with an unnecessary top-heavy management structure that included separate boards and CEO's for both the holding company and the bank. The sense of separate missions for the bank and the holding company's real estate subsidiary created internal confusion and strained the organizations limited resources.

In addition, the sense of mission at the bank seemed to dominate the bank's credit decisions and loan losses exceeded the original projections. Board leadership addressed these difficulties and a more consolidated and better-organized structure emerged.

Metro Bank has been served by an outstanding board of directors that, over time, has included regional bank executives from PNC and BB&T; executives from Louisville's local banks; executives from major business such as Brown-Forman, RJ Reynolds, General Electric and UPS; officials from Metro Government, and business leaders from the designated market area. The board included a balanced mix of African-American leadership, including individuals from the firms listed and from the local community. This very small bank has been very fortunate to have a very diversified and high quality board of directors over the past twenty years.

Metro Bank is classified as a Community Development Financial Institution [CDFI] and is tasked with a mission to stimulate economic growth within distressed neighborhoods. To accomplish its mission, the bank is committed to ensuring that the majority of its operations are within specific underserved communities or low-income census tracts in Jefferson County.

Being a CDFI allows the bank to participate in various CDFI Fund programs. The CDFI Fund was created in 1994 for the purpose of promoting economic revitalization and community development through investment in and assistance to community development financial institutions. The CDFI Fund's mission is to expand the capacity of financial institutions to provide credit, capital and financial services to underserved populations and communities in the United States.

Metro Bank participates in the Bank Enterprise Award Program [BEA Program]. The CDFI Fund provides monetary awards to FDIC-insured depository institutions, such as Metro Bank, that successfully demonstrate an increase in their own lending, investing, or service activities in distressed communities. Without these BEA Programs it would have been difficult for Metro Bank to operate profitably and continue to serve its designated market.

The Park DuValle neighborhood redevelopment was one of the original projects undertaken by LDB holding company through its real estate development subsidiary.

The Park DuValle project replaced more than 1,500 units of federally assisted affordable housing that were constructed in a 1950's slum clearance program. The poorly oriented building footprints separated these public housing developments from the surrounding neighborhood. Deferred maintenance had taken its toll over the succeeding three decades, and the developments became increasingly dilapidated and distressed. Crime was a serious problem and Louisville's west end had the most police reports per square mile in the State of Kentucky.

The new Park DuValle neighborhood project was a $200 million investment of public and private funds covering 125 acres that was once dominated by these public housing units. The Park DuValle neighborhood has been transformed into a mixed-income neighborhood in Louisville's west end. The goal was to build a series of traditional neighborhoods with rental and home ownership opportunities for a wide range of income groups.

The greatest challenge was to successfully provide public housing for those in need while simultaneously attracting middle-income homebuyers to the neighborhood. The Master Plan for the effort tied in adjacent communities with a new commercial center for shops and services for the residential neighborhoods.

The Villages of Park DuValle is now recognized by the US Department Housing & Urban Development [HUD] as one of the most outstanding examples of neighborhood revitalization in the nation. The Villages consist of single-family homes, duplexes, triplexes, fourplexes, sixplexes, townhouses, a 59-unit senior building, and over 5,500 square feet of commercial space. There are one, two, three, and four bedroom units, some of which are wheelchair accessible/adaptable.

The Park DuValle project represents a new approach to public housing: private construction, management, and ownership with public housing rental units located within market-rate rental and homeownership units. The project includes public services that low-income households need and amenities middle-income households expect.

The New Markets Tax Credit [NMTC] Program is another important CDFI Program for LDB and Metro Bank. The NMTC allocations are awarded to LDB and Metro Bank serves as the manager of the program.

LDB received its first NMTC allocation from the CDFI Fund in 2004 in the amount of $62.5 million. Subsequent allocations include: 2005 $8 million, 2008 $40 million and 2010 $14 million for a total of $124.5 million. The NMTC's are utilized by private business to help finance new facilities and create new jobs.

Metro Bank and the projects that have been undertaken to improve the west end neighborhoods have produced positive results. The concept of public-private partnerships has produced new housing and new jobs for residents of these distressed neighborhoods.

Bank regulators perform regular Community Reinvestment Act [CRA] examinations to insure that banks adequately serve their community. Metro Bank's CRA area was limited to certain zip codes in the west end of Louisville; it did not include downtown.

To our surprise, Metro Bank failed an early CRA exam because too many loans had been made in downtown to businesses that provided jobs for residents of the west end. The bank's local CDFI mission and federal CRA requirements did not match.

It's difficult for me to focus on any one individual in this chapter as many people have contributed to this success over the past 20 years. The dedication of the early organizers produced an organization that with the support of the CDFI Fund has been able to fulfill its mission under the leadership of Pedro Bryant, the Bank's President & CEO for the past fourteen years. Lori Elam CPA, the Bank's Chief Financial Officer, also deserves credit for her management contribution.

In retrospect, the most import contributions to the organization were made by some of the directors from the neighborhood. Individuals like Tony French had an in-depth understanding of the people and the needs of their neighborhoods. Their candid observations were an essential ingredient to my understanding of the issues we needed to address by working together. In my opinion, government programs won't work without including such "boots on the ground" community leadership.

After sixteen years, I resigned from my advisory board position with LDB in 2013 as a step toward reducing the number of business commitments that require regular travel.

Chapter Nine

CogenAmerica

In 1996, an investment group asked me if I would be interested in joining the board of directors of CogenAmerica, as an "independent director". This was another business being acquired out of bankruptcy and the bankruptcy court was requiring CogenAmerica to establish a special committee of independent directors to comply with the ownership regulations for electric utilities.

CogenAmerica was headquartered in Minneapolis, Minnesota, and, despite the cold winter weather; I accepted the invitation to join the board as an independent director.

Formerly O'Brien Environmental Energy, CogenAmerica emerged from bankruptcy in 1996, under a plan of reorganization proposed by NRG Energy, a subsidiary of Northern States Power. Under the plan of reorganization, NRG Energy owned 45% of CogenAmerica's common stock with the balance owned by public shareholders.

CogenAmerica's common stock was listed on NASDAQ at an opening price of $5.38 per share and the plan of reorganization established an Independent Directors Committee [IDC] to be responsible for managing the relationship with NRG Energy.

CogenAmerica was an independent power producer engaged primarily in the business of developing, owning and managing the operation of cogeneration projects, which produce electricity and thermal energy for sale under long-term contracts with industrial and commercial users and public utilities.

CogenAmerica had domestic natural gas fired cogeneration facilities located at:

- Greys Ferry - Philadelphia, Pennsylvania; 150 megawatts
- Parlin, New Jersey; 122 megawatts
- Morris, Illinois; 177 megawatts
- Pryor, Oklahoma; 110 megawatts
- Newark, New Jersey; 58 megawatts
- Philadelphia, Pennsylvania; 22 megawatts

CogenAmerica's international operations included Puma, a United Kingdom subsidiary, which designed and assembled power generation systems for the international market.

The ownership and board structure of CogenAmerica proved to be a very difficult arrangement to manage. NRG, with four board members, acted as if their ownership position permitted them to dictate policy; whereas, regulatory requirements prevented such control.

The eight-person board consisted of the four NRG directors, three independent directors [IDC members] and the independent Chief Executive Officer [CEO]. The IDC provided the check and balance to comply with the regulatory requirements. The court ordered company bylaws provided the legal roadmap for governance but executive sessions of the board without the CEO created a voting imbalance.

In my view, the most challenging board issue was compensation and I served as Chair of the board's Compensation Committee. NRG, a wholly owned subsidiary of an electric utility, had been created to participate in the rapidly deregulating electric power industry. Enron was, at that time, the leading company in this emerging deregulated electric power business.

Enron was not only changing the market for sales and distribution of electric power but was also changing the way executives were compensated. In addition to high salaries, Enron had also introduced very lucrative stock-based incentive compensation plans for Enron executives.

Enron's introduction of stock-based incentive compensation plans was as disruptive as the regulatory changes. Executives in the deregulated arena felt entitled to stock-based plans that offered significant upside potential; whereas, executives at traditional utilities did not participate in meaningful stock-based incentive compensation plans.

NRG was wholly owned by a traditional utility. NRG's executives had only modest cash incentives and no stock-based incentives at NRG. NRG's executives were not NRG shareholders and owned only a few shares in the parent utility.

CogenAmerica was a public company and our new President & CEO's compensation plan included stock options. The members of the IDC represented shareholders and, as board members, we were also compensated with a mix of cash and stock options.

As Chair of the Compensation Committee, I was surprised when the Committee's compensation consultant presented an incentive compensation plan for CogenAmerica's business development officers that provided for an immediate cash payout calculated on the "projected" cash flows from new power plant investments. Under the proposed terms the development officers would make the projections used to calculate their own incentive payout. In essence, the proposed plan was designed to permit the development officers to calculate their own cash bonus!

When I objected, the compensation consultant informed me that this plan was based on acceptable fair value accounting policy and was standard practice at Enron. We did not adopt this plan.

> *"The spirit of envy can destroy;*
> *it can never build."*
>
> *Margaret Thatcher*

CogenAmerica's operating and financial performance over the next year was excellent and the stock tripled in value. This stock price increase created unvested value in excess of $1.0 million in the new CEO's stock option plan. This increase in potential value clearly upset the four board members from NRG; I called it "option envy".

Even though CogenAmerica's financial performance was excellent the board entered a dysfunctional phase that resulted in a 4 to 3 vote to terminate the CEO during an executive session. The board members from NRG then insisted on naming a new CEO from the ranks of NRG, however, this required the consent of the independent directors on the IDC.

The first candidates proposed by NRG were not acceptable to the IDC. We reached a compromise with NRG on the selection of Julie Jorgensen, an attorney at NRG that had worked with the IDC on a variety of projects. The members of the IDC all respected Jorgensen and we were confident she had the skills required to manage the company.

As Chair of the Compensation Committee it was my job to help design a compensation package acceptable to NRG but retain a stock option component acceptable to Jorgensen. In the end, we agreed on a package that had a significant number of stock options vest at a price of $25.00 per share, a price that the NRG board members apparently thought was unattainable.

Jorgensen did an outstanding job as President & CEO and our confidence and respect for her was rewarded. However, the arrangement with NRG remained dysfunctional and it became clear would remain unworkable. As a result, the full board decided it was best to hire an investment banker to sell the company. To avoid a conflict of interest with NRG, the bankruptcy plan required the Independent Directors Committee to be given full control of the acquisition process.

Calpine Corporation acquired CogenAmerica in December 1999 for $25.00 per share in cash. We had several companies making offers to acquire the company and I received a call from a NRG director requesting that the IDC accept another offer for $24.99 in cash. Accepting a lower cash offer was not acceptable and we proceeded with the Calpine transaction.

Now, you might ask, why the $24.99 request? In my view, the answer was simple; Jorgensen's $25.00 stock options would not vest and she would not receive the additional $1.0 million+ option payout she was due at the $25.00 price.

In most respects, CogenAmerica was my most difficult board due to "option envy". Lesson learned; make certain every member of your board and management team is aligned for the benefit of the shareholders, not just their personal self-interest.

Looking back, I accepted the CogenAmerica board position because the company was operating in a deregulating industry that was growing by acquisition – similar to banking. However, I soon learned there was a significant difference.

The construction or acquisition of a new power plant with fixed electrical output was a one-time event. The deregulated power industry did not have the same opportunity to produce organic growth from an acquisition as the banking industry. Continued growth in earnings required new construction or acquisitions to be funded by borrowed money. Continued earnings growth was dependent on continued access to the capital markets.

In addition, longer-term earnings were subject to changing market conditions as electric distribution and pricing was now deregulated. Much of the industry's cost structure was fixed but the price of the power sold was subject to market conditions. The objective was to "lock in" cost and price for a period of time under contract but long-term profitability was still subject to market conditions.

Jorgensen did an excellent job of managing CogenAmerica's initial expansion but continued expansion required more capital or more debt. This was the same situation that faced NRG, Calpine and Enron. Within a few years each of these companies encountered financial challenges that resulted in bankruptcy protection.

Lesson learned; make certain you understand all significant long-term risk factors of the firm's business model and how these risks impact the firm's balance sheet, earnings, liquidity and capital structure.

Looking back we were fortunate that Jorgensen provided the leadership required for CogenAmerica to navigate the early growth phase and position the company for acquisition. We had the right management, timing of the sale was fortuitous and cash, rather than an exchange of shares, was the right price.

The operating and financial performance of CogenAmerica was excellent and the stock price increased from $5.00 to $25.00 in a three-year period with shareholder's receiving a five-fold return on their investment.

Option envy might just have forced the sale of CogenAmerica at the right time!

Chapter Ten

Republic Bank

Republic Bank, headquartered in St. Petersburg, Florida, initiated a national telemarketing program for non-traditional mortgage products during the 1990's. Republic discontinued this program following a significant increase in non-performing loans and the bank incurred a significant loss in 1998.

Republic's board of directors terminated a number of key officers, including the bank's Chief Executive Officer [CEO], and bank regulators placed the bank under a regulatory order that required the addition of new capital. The bank was operating with an interim CEO selected from the board.

The bank's investment bankers approached Keefe Partners and other investors about a potential investment. Keefe retained Chartwell to conduct due diligence. Our due-diligence concluded the credit issues could be resolved and the bank could return to profitability following a recapitalization.

We found it interesting that a Florida based bank located in what was considered one of the best real estate markets in the county decided it was better to operate a national telemarketing non-traditional mortgage-lending program. Looking back, the credit files and losses on the mortgage loans generated by this nationwide program should have offered me an early warning sign for the financial crisis of 2007-2009.

> *"It is not often that [people] learn from the past,*
> *even rarer that they draw the correct conclusions from it."*
>
> **Henry Kissinger**

Lessons were learned from the management issues associated with the earlier Arizona bank investment by Keefe Partners. As a result, this investment by Keefe Partners was contingent on the board of directors promptly initiating an executive search to identify and hire an experienced banking executive as Republic's new CEO.

In 1999, Republic completed a private placement of subordinated debentures. Keefe Partners participated in the private placement and Republic's board of directors added me to the bank's board.

It's important to note that Harry Keefe fully recognized the confidential nature of my board position. Once I became a board member at Republic he never asked me questions about the company and we never discussed matters at Republic.

The board organized a search committee [I was a member] and we initiated a search for a new CEO. In early 2000, Republic announced the election of William Klich as President & CEO.

Klich had a proven track record of resolving credit problems, improving operations and producing solid financial results. He had resolved similar problems at his previous bank and a large out-of-state regional bank had recently acquired the bank. Klich was now managing Florida operations for the out-of-state bank.

Once on board, Klich initiated a number of strategic initiatives including; the formation of a new management team, the exit from national market lending, a renewed concentration on Florida's market, new credit underwriting standards, and a repositioning of the bank's branch distribution system. At year-end 2003, prior to its acquisition by BB&T, Republic operated 71 full-service branches in 17 counties throughout Florida.

This is a short chapter as Republic had a well functioning board with a variety of skill sets and quality membership. Klich recruited a first class management team that worked together as a team.

Most important, Klich understood the Florida real estate market. Florida, like most of the country, was experiencing another real estate "boom" period. A number of out-of-state banks were very active in the high-rise condo market across Florida, especially South Florida.

In 2002, Klich and I were attending a meeting in a building where we could look out across the skyline of Miami. Klich looked at me and said; "too many construction cranes". As a result, Republic significantly reduced new commitments to real estate development in south Florida. Klich's judgment and experience were instrumental in helping Republic avoid the worst of the financial crisis.

Republic had also participated with a number of other banks in loans to mortgage brokers around the country. Klich began to exit these relationships and had reduced the bank's exposure to one remaining loan to a mortgage broker in Tampa, Florida. A few days before the loan was scheduled to pay off the bank was notified payment would not occur – fraud had been uncovered.

The discovery of fraud created an insurance claim for recovery by the bank. My previous experience with large multi-million dollar insurance claims was repeated at Republic. The bank starts a multi-step process that involves investigation, analysis of coverage, negotiation, litigation, expert witnesses and finally a check. In my experience, receiving payment is not easy.

My previous experience included a bank client that in the 1990's asked me to serve as an expert witness on an insurance claim. A bank officer had made an error on the redemption of a bond and, when corrected, the bank had incurred a loss of about $1.0 million. In this case the insurance company followed a path of delay – delay – delay. The bank's law firm neglected to follow required procedures and the insurance company then claimed the statute of limitations voided the banks claim.

The question on the table was "when did the loss occur?" I took the position that the loss occurred when the bank's regulators and accountants required the loss to be recorded on the bank's financial statements. This date was several years after the actual error was discovered.

Fortunately for my client, the insurance company's expert witness was a certified public accountant for a large firm and under cross-examination agreed that financial statements must reflect a loss when it occurs and confirmed the bank had recorded the loss properly. The judge ruled in my client's favor and the insurance company paid the claim.

In four years Klich had turned Republic into a well-managed profitable bank that had become a desirable banking franchise for larger out-of-state banks that were searching for an entry into the Florida market.

At the same time, Republic's largest individual shareholder who owned about 30% of the company's shares was increasingly interested in realizing the value that Klich had created for all shareholders as the stock had tripled in value.

The timing looked right to explore the potential acquisition of Republic by one of the interested out-of-state institutions. The board's first step was to identify and select the team of advisors to help guide the process.

The sale of a bank is a one-time event and it's important that the board conduct the process in a professional manner with the right advisors. The Republic board selected KBW as its investment banker and Ed Herlihy from Wachtell Lipton as its legal advisor.

As we expected, this team did an excellent job of identifying and evaluating potential acquirors, initiating discussions and then negotiating a final acquisition agreement with BB&T Corporation, headquartered in Winston-Salem, North, Carolina.

Republic, with $3.0 billion in assets, was the largest independent commercial bank in Florida when it was acquired by BB&T Corporation in 2004. BB&T, with $90 billion in assets at that time, was the nation's 9th largest bank.

Klich became Florida President for BB&T, served as President of the Florida Banker's Association, and he was a speaker at the Bank Directors Workshop hosted by the American Association of Bank Directors. After his retirement from BB&T we have worked together on a couple of Chartwell projects.

Selecting the right acquisition partner is essential when part of the consideration is paid with the stock of the acquiring company. Shareholders can certainly decide to sell the shares they receive in the transaction but the board of directors still has a responsibility to conduct due-diligence of the acquiror.

The 2007-09 financial crisis separated the strong from the weak and BB&T weathered the crisis. Readers of the CogenAmerica chapter will note that acquisition was for cash and Calpine, the acquiror, entered bankruptcy a few years after the transaction was competed.

Chapter Eleven

MainSource Financial Group

This MainSource chapter will be short as I am still a member of the board of directors and do not serve as an official spokesperson for this public company. MainSource Financial Group is a $4.0 billion asset financial institution headquartered in Greensburg, Indiana, with branch locations in Indiana, Illinois, Ohio and Kentucky.

In 2010, Archie Brown, President & CEO of MainSource Financial Group, contacted Chartwell about undertaking a board assessment. Following an interview by the bank's Governance Committee, Chartwell was retained to evaluate the board and committee structure and to recommend a board member to replace the company's retiring non-executive Chairman.

Chartwell's recommendations were accepted and [1] the board membership of both the holding company and the bank were reconstituted with substantially identical membership, [2] the boards were scheduled to meet on the same day, [3] the company elected Brian Crall as Lead Director and [4] the board organized a new board Risk Committee.

"Be a yardstick of quality"
Steve Jobs

The following year the Governance Committee approached me about joining the MainSource board of directors. Based on my confidence in Brown as the CEO [he expects excellence] and the integrity of this board, I accepted. For the past couple of years I have served as Chairman of the Nominating & Governance Committee [Nom/Gov].

Nom/Gov conducts an annual board and individual board member assessment with the assistance of an outside review every several years. The membership of the board is driven by a skills matrix to insure that the company has a mix of necessary talent on the board. In addition we have recruited three new board members over the past five years to replace retiring board members.

Nom/Gov is sensitive to the benefits of having diverse views and experience on the board. New board members represent a global medical equipment and services provider, a large health insurance company and an individual with financial services experience. Two of the last three board member additions are women.

In addition to Chair of Nom/Gov I serve as a member on the Risk Committee and the Executive Committee. My confidence in the management team and other board members has certainly been rewarding over the past five years and this has been a productive and very enjoyable relationship.

Brian Crall has exhibited excellent leadership skills as Lead Director and Archie Brown is a well-respected and effective CEO. These are the attributes anyone should look for before joining any board, especially a financial services company where board members have additional regulatory liability.

In early February 2016, MainSource had announced my plans not to stand for reelection at the company's annual meeting in April. My plans were changed when the board asked me to remain another year following Crall's announcement that he would not stand for reelection as a result of a potential conflict of interest with a new client at his firm.

At the board's request, I resubmitted my name for inclusion in the MainSource proxy and was reelected to the board by the shareholders at the annual meeting. I was unanimously elected Lead Director at the board meeting following the annual shareholder's meeting.

My goal for this year is to develop a smooth transition plan for my successor as Lead Director and, I am pleased to say, MainSource has a quality board with several qualified candidates.

Chapter Twelve

Cystic Fibrosis Foundation

Maurice Johnson, Chairman & CEO of Citizens Fidelity Bank, also set the stage in 1975 for my long-term commitment to working with the Cystic Fibrosis Foundation [CFF] when he asked me to stop by his office and suggested it was time for me to have some "community involvement". He asked if I would be interested in joining the board of a local charitable organization and a few days later indicated the Kentucky-West Virginia Chapter of Cystic Fibrosis was interested in having a board member from Citizens.

Cystic Fibrosis [CF] is a progressive genetic disorder that causes persistent lung infections and limits the ability to breathe over time. A defective gene causes a thick buildup of mucus in the lungs, pancreas and other organs. In the lungs, the mucus clogs the airways and traps bacteria leading to infections, extensive lung damage and eventually, respiratory failure. CFF medical research has contributed to significant CF drug development over the past several decades but there is currently no cure for Cystic Fibrosis.

My involvement with CFF includes my election to the national board of trustees in 1980 and will have spanned over forty years when my term as a Trustee of the national CF Foundation ends in 2017. My involvement with CFF includes working with a remarkable number of exceptional people dedicated to raising money for research and finding a cure for this fatal genetic disorder.

"We make a living by what we get,
we make a life by what we give."

Sir Winston Churchill

In the late 1970's, I was elected President of the Kentucky/West Virginia Chapter a position that tended to rotate among board members every couple of years. At this time individual Chapters were fairly independent and hired their own Executive Directors and managed their own fund raising programs with an expectation that excess funds would be sent to national headquarters. Our chapter's largest fundraiser was a Celebrity

Dinner Party hosted by Pee Wee Reese, the retired major league baseball player.

A few weeks before the 1979 fundraiser, the chapter's Executive Director came to my office at the bank and announced he was resigning to lead another local charity. When I asked about his staff he indicated that both staff members were joining him at the new charity. I expressed surprise and disappointment that he had made such a decision just a few weeks before our most important event and arranged to conduct exit interviews with each of his two assistants.

After a few minutes of conversation it became clear his senior assistant had a long-term allegiance to the Executive Director and was going to follow him to the new charity. Further conversation was a waste of time.

My meeting with Richard Mattingly, hired a few months earlier as the chapter's junior fundraiser, was more promising. At the conclusion of our meeting I told Mattingly if he could organize and manage a successful Celebrity Dinner Party in just a few weeks time then I would select him as the chapter's new Executive Director. If, on the other hand, he did not think that was possible then he should join the other two departing employees.

Mattingly elected to stay, managed a very successful event and under his leadership our chapter became one of the best performers in the country.

In 1980, the national CF Foundation was undergoing dramatic change as it was attempting to become better organized and managed. At that time, the national organization was basically a clearinghouse to fund limited medical research with money raised by local chapters. The national board of trustees had decided to reach out and recruit new trustees from the business community to help structure a more businesslike organization. Based on my banking and financial experience, I was approached and accepted a position as a national Trustee.

During my first board meeting it was clear the national CF Foundation needed to be better organized and managed. My decision to join CFF as a Trustee was strongly influenced by the parents of children with Cystic Fibrosis who served as Trustees.

These CF parents could not have been more dedicated and sincere about doing what was necessary to cure this fatal genetic disorder that had been inherited by their children. It was an infectious atmosphere and I was hooked.

Richard Dandurand, another non-parent and a partner in a national CPA firm, was also approached and recruited as a new Trustee in 1980 and we have served together for the past 36 years. In many respects Dandurand has been the conscience of the Foundation making certain to ask if we are spending enough on research and keeping everyone focused on our goal of curing Cystic Fibrosis. As the foundation has grown Dandurand has been instrumental in consistently upgrading financial controls and asking the tough questions required to protect the Foundation's financial and public integrity.

A change in the CF Foundation's leadership also occurred in the early 1980's and the Foundation became much more businesslike in its operations. The individual chapters were reorganized and consolidated under the national Foundation. The Foundation's efficiency improved and fundraising began to increase.

The most important new addition to national staff in 1980 was the hiring of Dr. Robert Beall as the Foundation's new Medical Research Director. At that time, CFF had big dreams but an annual medical budget of only $4.0 million. CF was a kids' disease with an average life span of less than 18 years of age. Beall's vision would lead to dramatic changes in both medical research and the business model for medical research over the next 35 years.

The national office recognized Mattingly's success in Kentucky and he accepted a fundraising position on the national staff in 1983. Mattingly helped restructure nationwide fundraising by identifying successful events at individual chapters that could be introduced as new nationwide events. In addition, new programs were introduced to raise money from large donors. This increase in funding helped to significantly expand CFF's medical research programs.

In 1982, the Foundation created its first Research Development Program, a national program to help fund an interdisciplinary network of research centers to accelerate understanding of CF and the complexities of the disease.

The 1980's were a remarkable time for both CF research and clinical care. At the start of the decade scientists knew very little about the CF gene. A major breakthrough was achieved in 1989 when the CF gene was discovered by research teams headed by Professor Lap-Chi Tsui, Dr Francis Collins and Professor Jack Riordan. Dr Collins is currently the Director of the National Institutes of Health the Federal Government's medical research organization.

The discovery of the CF gene was met with great hope for the discovery of a cure, a hope that as of today is unfulfilled. It's an understatement to say that genetic science is exceedingly complex and, although research has made great strides in the treatment of CF, a cure remains in the distant future.

Treatments for CF also improved during the 1980's and early 1990's. However, not all local pharmacies would carry drugs for a rare genetic disease such as CF. In response, the Foundation organized a CF pharmacy in 1988 with the objective of delivering specialty drugs by mail order to CF patients at the lowest possible cost and assisting CF patients with obtaining insurance coverage to pay for CF drugs.

The IRS required the CF pharmacy to be a for-profit subsidiary of the CF Foundation. I served as its Chairman of the Board for about 10 years. In this role I learned a significant amount about the dysfunction of our nation's health and insurance system. For example, when reviewing the CF Pharmacy's staff it was clear that the ratio of patient support staff to pharmacists was about ten to one. We had ten times the number of people dealing with insurance and access to drugs than people actually filling prescriptions for CF patients.

Delivery, cost and payment challenges continue to increase following the successful development, approval and delivery of new CF drugs. The health insurance system continues to undergo significant change and, in response, the CF pharmacy was sold to Walgreens in 2012. CFF programs for CF patient services and assistance are being continuously expanded by the Foundation.

Beall was elevated to President of CFF in 1994 and he has been responsible for twenty-one years of exceptional leadership in medical research. Beall assembled an executive management team that provided solid leadership for several decades, a rare feat in any field. Mattingly had been promoted to Chief Operating Officer, Vera Twigg served as Chief Financial Officer and Preston Campbell MD joined CFF in 1998 to head CFF's medical research activities. The record established by this team on all fronts is simply amazing and clearly demonstrates the benefit to any organization of having the best people working together to achieve a common goal.

Frank Deford served as Chairman of the Foundation for much of the 1990's. A eloquent speaker and writer, Deford had written a book, "Alex", [TV Movie in 1986] about his daughters struggle with Cystic Fibrosis.

CF board meetings are entirely focused on business and little or no time is devoted to personal visits. I have served for years without knowing any significant personal information about my fellow Trustees.

One evening after a meeting as Deford and I were walking together back to the hotel he was stopped by several people asking for his autograph! So – I asked, "Who are you?" Deford responded "they probably recognized me from TV."

My friends know I am not a spectator sports fan and seldom watch TV. I had "known" Deford for years and did not realize he was a senior writer at Sports Illustrated, was host of a morning sports show on National Public Radio, frequent host of TV sports events and now the author of fifty books. I just knew Deford as a CF parent that had lost his daughter.

__"What touches me is that so many caring people have signed on to this battle simply out of the goodness of their hearts. I always stand in the shadow of their nobility, in the greatest of gratitude, because we families who have been cursed with CF cannot win this fight alone."__

__Frank Deford__

Beall also wanted more direct involvement in finding treatments for Cystic Fibrosis beyond the Foundation's traditional approach of funding basic research for "orphan diseases" at universities. Beall's vision is now referred to as "venture philanthropy".

His objective was for CFF to encourage CF drug development by helping fund CF drug discovery and development at biotech and pharmaceutical firms with promising ideas. Such funding by CFF was to support drug development and a byproduct would be potential royalties received on sales of any drug CFF funded that received FDA approval and made it to market.

The unusual nature of CFF's arrangements would attract initial skepticism and criticism from other non-profit medical research organizations. History has validated Beall's approach as it has produced life-changing drugs for people with CF.

In the late 1990's, Beall asked the Trustees for authority to help fund the discovery and development of potential CF drugs at small California biotechnology firm named Aurora Biosciences. Aurora's drug candidates were intended to address the underlying cause of CF.

This "investment" would be the first of Beall's new approach of funding biotech and pharmaceutical research to help identify, develop and deliver new CF drugs to CF patients. As described later, Beall's vision would pay significant "dividends" to help fund even more research in future years.

In 2002, the Board of Trustees embarked on a mission to provide more effective governance for a growing organization. At that time the board consisted of forty-six Trustees. The board's Executive Committee, consisting of a dozen Trustees, essentially governed the organization. This process to improve governance was lead by Catherine McLoud, CFF Board Chair.

In a remarkable display of McLoud's leadership, at the 2003 Annual Meeting the CFF Board of Trustees voted to reduce the size of the board from forty-six to nineteen members and restructured committees were organized for audit, investment and governance. McLoud demonstrated great skill in working with all Trustees to accomplished this reorganization without a dissenting vote at the Annual Meeting. I still think it's amazing that the majority of existing Trustees voted to eliminate their position on the CFF Board.

In 2012, a CF drug based on the initial CFF funding at Aurora was approved by the FDA and made available to CF patients. Beall's approach had helped fund the research that resulted in the first drug to treat the underlying cause of CF. The fact that it took almost thirteen years from initial funding to market introduction clearly illustrates the time and cost it takes to bring a new drug to market.

In 2014, CFF negotiated the sale of the future royalty stream from new and future CF drugs from one biotech firm to a royalty investment fund for $3.3 billion. CFF's sale of the royalty stream will now provide funding for even more research, drug development and clinical trials for even better CF drugs. Over time, Beall's vision of venture philanthropy has provided over $3.7 billion of additional funding to help CFF pursue its mission to find a cure for CF.

In 2014, CFF uncovered alleged misconduct by an employee that worked for Mattingly and the employee was notified an investigation would be undertaken. The following day a senseless tragedy stuck when, according to police, the employee visited Mattingly's home, killed Mattingly's wife and the employee subsequently died of a self-inflicted gunshot. Words cannot describe the shock and terrible impact these horrible events had on Mattingly and the entire CF community.

Ultimately, Mattingly elected to retire from CFF and organize a new non-profit dedicated to workplace mental health. Mattingly contributed greatly to the success of CFF for thirty-seven years and it is exceptionally sad that such a successful career ended in such a senseless and tragic manner. Frankly, it's difficult for me to share these tragic events, as I consider both Rich Mattingly and his wife, Carolyn, as personal friends.

In 2015, Beall retired as President after thirty-six years with CFF and twenty-two years as its President and CEO. Preston Campbell succeeded Beall as President and CEO and we look forward to continued medical achievements under his stewardship. Campbell had assembled a first class medical research team and the Foundation was well positioned for a smooth leadership transition.

It has been my pleasure to serve on CFF's investment committee for several decades, much of this time as its Chairman. CFF is also an amazing financial story when you consider that during my time as a Trustee CFF's medical budget has grown from $4.0 million to $164 million per year and fund's available for future research have increased from essentially zero to over $3.0 billion. But most important is the fact that today the majority of CF patients have access to drugs that treat the underlying cause of CF and the average survival age is now over forty. The majority of CF patients have now grown to adults.

There are simply too many people who have contributed to CFF to mention in this chapter. CFF's management and Trustees, past and present, are a remarkable group of dedicated and talented individuals. I remain in awe of the medical talent devoted to finding a cure for Cystic Fibrosis. The parents and the children [many now adults] with CF I have met over the years have my utmost admiration for the courage they display.

However, medical research has not found a cure and CF still prematurely takes the lives of people with this genetic defect. I was reminded of the critical importance of CFF's search for a cure when I attended the recent funeral for McLoud's 34-year-old son.

It's been my privilege to serve and my modest contribution is over shadowed by the efforts and dedication of others in the CF family. CF Trustees are a dedicated group of individuals that in addition to making financial contributions donate their time and talent without financial compensation or reimbursement of travel expenses. CFF has been my longest serving relationship; however, after 36 years as a Trustee I have announced that I will not stand for reelection at CFF's 2017 Annual Meeting.

Johnson was correct; it was time for some "community involvement". This book contains numerous chapters describing business events; however, I remain most proud of my small part in contributing to healthier and longer lives for people with Cystic Fibrosis.

Chapter Thirteen

American Bankers Association

The American Bankers Association [ABA] is a Washington, DC, based trade association for the US banking industry. Founded in 1875, ABA represents financial institutions of all sizes and charters.

Like many large trade associations, ABA's principal activities include lobbying, professional development for member institutions, maintenance of best practices and industry standards, consumer education, and distribution of products and services. ABA is considered the largest financial institutions trade group in the United States.

Citizens Fidelity was an ABA member and in 1978 I was invited to join the ABA Accounting Task Force. The Task Force had about a dozen members who were appointed for staggered three-year terms. The members tended to be either the Chief Accounting Officer [CAO] or the Chief Financial Officer [CFO] of their respective banks. Joining this talented group provided an opportunity for me to develop informal relationships with the other members during our periodic meetings in Washington.

The Task Force would have regular formal meetings to exchange views with representatives from all bank regulators, the Securities & Exchange Commission [SEC] and the Financial Accounting Standards Board [FASB]. Being involved with the ABA certainly gave me a front row seat on industry-wide regulatory, financial and accounting developments.

The ABA also asked me to interface with certain legislators who served on congressional financial committees. I quickly learned this really meant meeting with congressional staff members who tended to be young and had little, if any, knowledge of financial services. It was clear that I was asked because, at age 34, I tended to be the youngest member of the Task Force and could theoretically better relate to congressional staff.

In 1981, I was asked to serve a fourth year and help lead an ABA project to address the adequacy of commercial bank loan loss reserves. The Task Force retained Arthur D Little [ADL] to conduct this study. At that time the tax code provided for a declining percentage of tax-deductible loan loss reserves. The ABA and many member banks were concerned that future provisions to the loan loss reserve would not be adequate during future periods of economic stress.

I will not attempt to describe ADL's complex analysis of tax code changes and the impact on future loan loss reserves addressed by their analysis. In the end, I doubt anyone in congress really understood the issue [remember I was meeting with young inexperienced staff] and periodic changes to the tax code have produced today's Deferred Tax Asset [DTA].

Bank earnings suffer when credit losses increase and, as the ADL analysis predicted, without sufficient earnings the value of the DTA would be subject to impairment. In certain circumstances the DTA would need to be eliminated and, therefore, reduce bank capital during a period of economic stress. This is what happened thirty years later during the 2007-2009 financial crisis.

An increasing number of the members of the Accounting Task Force were the CFO at their banks with responsibilities similar to mine that included more than accounting. Most of us also had responsibility for asset/liability management, investments and other matters. We proposed the ABA organize a new Chief Financial Officers Division that was established by the ABA in 1982.

In 1983, I was invited to join this new CFO Division and was selected its Chairman in 1985 for my final year. Don Howard, CFO of Citicorp was selected as my Vice Chairman and succeeded me as Chairman the following year.

My prior relationship with Howard certainly paid benefits that year as he provided staff at Citicorp to help me with the projects I wanted to undertake at ABA. I referred to 1985 as the year Howard worked for me and our relationship produced a very successful term for me. My thanks still go to Howard for that support.

The ABA also conducted a national banking school at Rutgers University and, although I never attended as a student, the ABA invited me to serve on the thesis faculty. Working with other faculty members, all senior officers at other banks, we would read a couple of thesis prepared by students from other banks and then interview and pass/fail each student as a panel.

The ABA also conducted a number of banking conferences and schools at other universities. From time to time I would be invited to speak at an ABA conference or conduct a class at the ABA Investment School.

Most of these classroom presentations would create a lively debate about the role of the investment portfolio. My philosophy of interest rate risk management to help provide steady earnings for the total bank frequently clashed with the view of bank portfolio managers that viewed their jobs as maximizing the return from their bank's investment portfolio.

Many such portfolio managers didn't appreciate my view that its easy to generate a higher return; you just take more credit risk or more price volatility risk by extending maturities. Both approaches improve yield but create more valuation risk during periods of economic stress and volatile interest rates.

This topic remains a matter of philosophy even today, however, in my experience most bank portfolio mangers that manage for yield will eventually pay the price for excessive volatility. More than one such manager has found himself or herself without a job when the markets turn against their position.

My relationship with a wide range of committee members at the ABA certainly expanded my horizons and provided me with a front row seat for the many challenges faced by the banking industry. This experience served me well when I later became Chairman of the American Association of Bank Directors.

Chapter Fourteen

American Association of Bank Directors

The American Association of Bank Directors [AABD], Washington, DC, was founded in 1989 in the midst of the S&L crisis to meet the information, education and advocacy needs of individual bank and savings institution directors. The AABD is the only banking trade association in the United States which exclusively serves individual directors rather than their financial institutions. David Baris, a Partner with the Buckley Sandler law firm in Washington, DC, serves as President of AABD.

I became acquainted with AABD and Baris when doing some governance research for a banking client in the early 2000's. Baris asked me to participate in a couple of AABD educational programs being hosted by state banking associations. I enjoyed making these presentations and meeting bankers and other bank directors at these banking conferences. As a speaker, I had complimentary access to all the other presentations. Needless to say, being invited to speak is a very cost effective way to gain new knowledge.

In 2007, AABD selected me as its new Chairman and I served in this capacity for five years until 2012. Baris and I worked together to expand AABD activities with community bank boards during the financial crisis. I recruited my son, Travis, to help upgrade the technology platform and digital marketing programs. Our efforts were rewarded as AABD online membership increased five-fold during this period.

AABD has limited staff and most educational programs are co-hosted with other banking organizations. During my term we co-hosted programs in a number of states and we were invited to speak at numerous banking conferences. AABD's relationships with the Western Independent Bankers Association [WIB] and the National Association of Corporate Directors [NACD] were especially important.

AABD worked with the WIB and its Executive Director, Nancy Sheppard, to host an Annual 3-day Bank Directors Conference. The success of this annual conference was due to Sheppard's leadership.

WIB also invited me to speak at a number of their other banking conferences. I recall speaking at one early morning session; my topic was "When Things Go Wrong", that didn't get off to a good start. I had posted a list of potential problems from recent news headlines on a screen in front of the room to discuss.

A rather rude [late party night?] individual interrupted my opening remarks with the following comment:

> "Why should we listen to you? What do you know about these topics?"

In response, I referred to the list I had posted and relied:

> "Scar-Tissue – unfortunately I have been involved with every type of situation listed and I haven't handled some of them very well."

The program then got underway with a good discussion about how things can go wrong and how a board should address difficult situations. At the conclusion, I received good ratings and it was an interactive and enjoyable session.

This was the first time I recall referring to "Scar-Tissue", but it has now become a frequent reference. I think too many speakers only talk about success and not mistakes. Most audiences seem to find it refreshing when I discuss a mistake and what I learned as a result.

WIB publishes the Directors Digest, a series of monthly articles for bank directors. In 2011, WIB invited me to submit a series of quarterly articles, which are included in Section II of this book.

AABD also co-hosted a Bank Directors Workshop for nine years with the National Association of Corporate Directors [NACD] in Florida. Great speakers are the key to quality programs and my relationships with both AABD and NACD was the key to getting great speakers from regulatory agencies and professional firms.

I have been asked and have enjoyed making presentations for many organizations across the country. Most organizations have participants' rate topics and speakers and the results can be very helpful. I seldom get the top score and frequently have someone who really didn't like my approach. Many, not all, such critical comments are actually very helpful and beneficial.

The best compliment I received during the financial crisis was the invitation to be the lead off speaker at the annual Financial Institutions Conference hosted by the Kentucky CPA Society for three consecutive years.

AABD also changed its approach to publishing AABD reports as a result of my experience with publishing my book, "*It Is What It Is*", describing how Pat Rusnak's leadership saved AmericanWest Bank from closure by the FDIC.

"*It Is What It Is*" was published using a self-publication service and it provided the format for future AABD publications. This approach permits AABD to prepare and publish a book that can be purchased online from Amazon [just like this book] and it is no longer necessary to print, store and ship books from the national office. This streamlined approach has helped AABD update, publish and distribute a number of important regulatory studies.

The most important aspect of my term as Chairman of AABD was consistent interaction with key regulators at the Federal Deposit Insurance Corporation, Comptroller of the Currency and the Federal Reserve Bank. These meetings with senior regulators gave Baris and myself the opportunity to exchange views with regulators about policies that impact community banks and their board members.

In 2008, I recall discussing the importance of liquidity with Sheila Bair, Chair of the FDIC, and leaving her office convinced she did not understand the negative consequences of the FDIC's policy on brokered CDs. Other meetings were much more constructive, however, I doubt our meetings had any material impact on regulatory policy.

These regulatory meetings did give me insight that proved helpful in helping my banking clients navigate the financial crisis. In addition, as all meetings are "on the record" I was also able to share some insight as a speaker at various banking conferences.

Both the St Louis Federal Reserve and the Cleveland Federal Reserve invited me to speak at regional banking conferences they hosted for community banks. At one such conference I had the "privilege" of being on the program with Elisabeth Warren [now a Senator from Massachusetts] during her time as interim head of the new Consumer Financial Protection Bureau [CFPB].

Warren and I sat together at the speakers' table and we had an opportunity to visit for several hours. I was disappointed that she could not name a single person with any banking experience on her staff. In addition, the email address she gave to me as the contact for community bankers did not work.

Warren's presentation was about her goal to simplify the mortgage application process and how it would be much better for both consumers and banks - with no negative impact on the banks in the room. She failed to understand that such a new form would require changes to the entire process; updated computer systems, new training programs, new regulatory compliance programs, etc.

The most interesting speaking invitation I received was an invitation to share my views at a joint conference of bank regulators hosted by the Conference of State Bank Supervisors. [CSBS]. Charles Vice, Banking Commissioner of Kentucky, was serving as Chair of the CSBS. Vice was also a speaker at the AABD's Bank Director Workshop on several occasions.

I could not attend the other regulatory sessions but I did visit with various regulators at lunch prior to my session. No slides, just a few opening remarks about being a bank director and then answering questions from bank regulators for about an hour. I was pleased that the regulators in the room were really interested in hearing the viewpoints of a bank director concerning the challenges facing community banking.

Some bankers might be disappointed that I did not list the increasing regulatory burden as the greatest long-term problem for community banks – I indicated my greatest concern was that all the negative publicity would discourage quality college graduates from entering the banking field. Quality people are necessary for any business to succeed.

My term as Chairman of AABD ended in 2012 and I now serve AABD as Chairman Emeritus.

Chapter Fifteen

National Association of Corporate Directors

In 2005, I was invited to meet with several representatives of the National Association of Corporate Directors [NACD] and local corporate directors to discuss organizing a new Florida Chapter of the NACD.

Embarrassed to say, the meeting did not get off to a good start. I was helping a mechanic on our boat that morning and was not dressed appropriately when my phone notified me I was due shortly at this meeting. After a very quick clean up, I drove to the downtown hotel.

Apparently Gerry Czarnecki, who became the chapter's first Chairman, and the other invited directors, appreciated my honesty about my "late arrival, casual attire and the distraction" and I was invited to be a founding board member of the new NACD Florida Chapter.

The NACD, headquartered in Washington, DC, is the nation's leading professional organization for corporate boards. As of 2016 the national organization provided exclusive resources, connections, and educational opportunities to more than 17,000 members.

The NACD Florida Chapter was organized in 2005 to conduct monthly educational programs for corporate directors during the Florida "season"; October to May.

The first orders of business were the selection of an Executive Director for the new chapter, identification and solicitation of sponsors to fund chapter operations, and identification of people to conduct the initial monthly programs in Fort Lauderdale.

Based on my introduction, the board selected my sister, Linda, as the new NACD Executive Director. To avoid any potential conflict of interest, I have not been active in management of the chapter. Linda announced her retirement in 2016 and I am proud that her leadership over the past eleven years helped the Florida chapter successfully expand from its original base in Fort Lauderdale to include programs in Miami, Naples and Tampa.

In my view, governance and administration of NACD Florida has resembled a typical non-profit volunteer board with very few board meetings and most of the work being done by the Executive Director. The success of the chapter today is based on Linda's work with a few energetic board members to select topics, identify speakers and organize monthly programs.

Most programs are scheduled for about 90 minutes in the early morning or late afternoon with time for attendees to visit before and after. This format provides time for a professional presentation and time for all participants to discuss the event and get to know one another. Not only is program content beneficial but I have also had the opportunity to meet and work with a number of Florida business leaders such as Bill Pruitt and Don Denkhaus who also serve as board members of NACD Florida.

Attendees rate every NACD program and I am pleased to say that Florida programs consistently receive ratings between 4.5 and 5.0 on a 5-point scale. The quality of programs has been largely due to support from chapter sponsors: Joe Mallin has conducted an annual compensation program, Lauren Smith has consistently organized quality programs, and David Walker has provided great leadership in the Tampa and Naples markets.

Florida is home to a large number of community banks and, in 2006, I arranged for the NACD Chapter to co-host the first Bank Directors Workshop [BDW] with the American Association of Bank Directors [AABD].

The annual BDW was a full-day program that included speakers from The Federal Reserve Bank, Federal Deposit Insurance Corporation, State of Florida, law firms, accounting firms, investment bankers with lunch keynotes from people like Mark Grant, a frequent guest on CNBC, Alex Sink, CFO of the State of Florida and Charles Vice, Chair of CSBS.

To be fair, I should list every speaker at the BDW as someone who helped me organize these programs over this nine-year period. I especially enjoyed doing joint presentations with Susan O'Donnell on executive compensation and with George Parkerson from the FDIC in Washington, DC.

As recognition of the national NACD has grown nationally, the organization has adopted new polices that limit co-hosted programs such as the BDW that invite board members who are not NACD members. As a result, we discontinued the BDW program in 2015. As Chair of the BDW during its nine-year history I was pleased that it consistently had the highest attendance of any NACD program in Florida. In addition, both the speakers and the program consistently achieved the highest ratings.

The national NACD office is also expanding services to its members to include board assessments and board search, services that compete with potential sponsors at the chapter level.

Another new policy that prevents program hosting by sponsors limits program evolvement and potential sponsor recruitment at the chapter level. It remains to be seen how these new national policies will impact the NACD chapters as sponsors have provided much of our core financial and program support.

The national NACD hosts a wide variety of excellent, but expensive, national programs. In 2014, I was asked to speak at the NACD's Master Class program in Florida and at the Masters Class in Arizona the following year. The NACD asked me to be a co-speaker at these programs with Ray Gilmartin, former Chairman & CEO of Merck & Co and former Lead Director of Microsoft. Full disclosure: Gilmartin consistently received [slightly] higher speaker ratings.

The Master Class Program is the final step in achieving NACD recognition as a Board Leadership Fellow, the highest standard of credentialing for corporate directors. These events are limited to fifty attendees and I had the opportunity to visit with an outstanding group of men and women corporate directors. An additional benefit for me was being able to attend these high quality programs and complete my requirements to be recognized as a Board Leadership Fellow.

I am certain I learned more from the attendees than they learned from me. In addition to Gilmartin, its rare to have the opportunity to visit with a former astronaut who walked on the moon, a female retired Coast Guard Admiral or the former head of cyber security for the Pentagon – to name a few.

The NACD offers first class educational programs and related professional materials to corporate board members. My association with NACD allows me to learn from excellent programs at both the chapter and national level and to meet outstanding people. However, NACD membership and programs are too expensive for many individuals, smaller companies and community banks.

Fortunately, many other organizations, such as the AABD, also offer board and governance education. I strongly recommend that anyone interested in joining a board identify a board organization that matches your needs, join that organization and participate in the organization's programs.

> *"Life is like a box of chocolates*
> *You never know what you're gonna get"*
>
> **Movie: Forrest Gump**

Section II

Publications & Articles

This section contains a wide range of articles that have been published by:

Directors & Boards Magazine

Directors Digest

The following organizations have published articles and interviews that have not been included but are listed below for reference:

American Banker Newspaper

2008   Viewpoint: Fair Value's Impact Will Only Grow
2006   Viewpoint: Regulatory Relief Legislation
2006   Interview: Regulatory Relief Article Interview
2003   Viewpoint: Fair Value Accounting & Stock Options

Corporate Board Member Magazine

2005   Interview: Director Liability
       Enron & Worldcom Settlements

2004   Interview: "What Directors Think" Issue
       Board Member Evaluations

2004   Interview: Living with Sarbanes-Oxley
       Board Member Risk

2003   Interview: "What Directors Think" Issue
       Life on the Wire & Director Responsibility

Section II

Publications & Articles

Cover: Directors & Boards Magazine 3Q2014

What we at *Directors & Boards* refer to as our "Jimmy Stewart" cover is the winner of a prestigious award. The American Society of Business Press Editors (ASBPE) awarded a silver medal in its national competition and a gold medal in its regional competition for the image we used for the cover story on "Joining a Bank Board: Should You Accept?" in the Third Quarter 2014 edition. (The image is actor Jimmy Stewart portraying troubled banker George Bailey in the movie classic "Is a Wonderful Life.")

Directors & Boards art director Monica McLaughlin was on hand to except the award – for: Design Excellence: Front Cover Photo – at the ASBPE's national conference. Founded in 1964, ASBPE is the professional association for full-time and freelance editors and writers employed in the business, trade and specialty press.

Charles J Thayer was the lead author of the "Joining a Bank Board" feature that inspired the winning cover design.

James Kristie
Editor
Directors & Boards

So, you've been invited to join a bank board

Should you accept?

In many respects the banking industry has become the favorite 'piñata' of politicians, the media and the public; everyone feels entitled to take a swipe. The recent financial crisis seriously damaged the image of the entire banking industry including the reputations of both bankers and bank directors.

Today over 5,000 regional and community banks serve customers and communities throughout our nation. These banks not only survived the crisis but the vast majority remained profitable and they continue to serve their communities through difficult times. All financial institutions may have been painted with the 'wall street' brush by the media but most community banks remain on solid footing and continue to work to support economic growth in their communities.

Serving as a board member of a community bank may have been considered an honor in the past - but times have changed. Accepting such a position today requires careful consideration. This article will explore some of the many pros and cons of serving on a bank board.

I believe the most significant challenge faced by banking today is attracting talented people to such an unpopular industry. Bank directors serve an important and unique role and it's especially important that community bank's attract and retain talented people on their boards. Hopefully, this article will help you decide if you should be one of those people.

The banking system provides the financial liquidity required to support our nation's economic and job growth. Some politicians don't seem to understand that our nation's banks provide the oil for our nation's economic engine and without oil an engine won't run. As a result, it's essential that the banking industry attracts and retains quality leadership in both day-to-day management and in the boardroom.

Community banks have a special relationship with 'small business' and economic analysis indicates that the majority of job growth is provided by small business. Community banks are best positioned to serve the financial needs of small business and are an essential contributor to future job growth throughout our nation.

The job of a community bank director comes with many risks and few personal rewards. Although this article will first address some of ugly aspects of serving as a bank director I believe it is a very worthwhile and rewarding position. I am privileged to serve on the board of a mid-west institution with banking locations in four states and have previously served on the boards of three other banking institutions of varying sizes.

My background also includes service as a financial executive at two regional banking institutions and additional board service at two non-financial companies. This article addresses the key elements of my decision process before I accepted each of these bank board positions and also before I declined invitations to join a few other bank boards.

Despite the risks I will describe, I encourage you to serve on a bank board that will benefit from your personal knowledge and skill set and that meets your personal due diligence requirements.

The American Association of Bank Directors [AABD] has recently updated an analysis that indicates over 800 bank regulatory rules and regulations apply to bank directors. Bank regulators have continually added new items to the job description of a bank director. The job of a bank director continues to become more complex with an increasing number of banking rules and regulations to consider in addition to the traditional fiduciary responsibilities required of all corporate directors.

Doing your personal due-diligence and gaining an understanding of the scope of regulatory requirements will help avoid surprises as you engage in bank board activities. Oversight of regulatory compliance is an essential part of a bank director's job but it is also a potential distraction to board oversight of corporate strategy and financial performance. As a result, bank boards tend to meet much more frequently than non-financial boards so be prepared for a substantial time commitment.

Your increased time commitment will not be offset by higher director compensation as national studies continue to report that community bank directors tend to be compensated at lower levels than board members of non-financial corporations of similar size. Don't expect to receive any significant compensation for your time commitment.

Also, expect your attorney to tell you this increased time commitment will be accompanied by more personal liability than board members of non-financial corporations due to a bank director's higher regulatory exposure. As a result, you will want to make certain the bank has a robust directors & officers insurance policy and by-law indemnification to protect you as much as possible.

In addition, you will see media reports about the Federal Deposit Insurance Corporation [FDIC] taking legal action to recover losses from bank officers and directors at failed banks. In my experience, such claims are generally made against board members because they approved loans that ultimately went bad. Therefore, I suggest you and other board members do not approve individual loans [except those required by bank regulation]. Make certain you fully understand how the bank's board and its committee structure functions by reading the bank's committee charters and talking to current board members.

However, the most important element of your due-diligence is to gain confidence in the ability and integrity of the bank's board members and management team. We all know that people are the key element that will make or break any business. Take the time to personally evaluate the other board members and gain an understanding of the bank's performance and the management team's strategy and abilities.

Your decision to be a bank director also requires some self-evaluation. A successful bank requires a quality mix of people and talent. Can you truly add value to the bank's board or do you duplicate existing skills? In my experience effective boards tend to be small with 8 to 12 members and every seat is important. Consider that you might not be the right person to occupy a seat even though the other board members may want you to join. This self-evaluation needs to be an ongoing process and you should also be prepared to recognize when its time for you to leave the board.

Accept the board seat only after you are comfortable with your duties as a bank director, the time commitment, the board structure and you have confidence in both the other board members and the management team. Over time you will be building personal and professional relationships with all of these people and they are the key to the bank's future success.

Once on board the challenge of being a bank director will be begin. No other business interacts with every other type of business in the communities served by your bank. Bank directors have a unique window into economic activity within their regional and local markets. Your bank's customer and credit strategy will have a direct impact on the lives and jobs of people throughout your markets.

Rapidly changing technology is changing the way bank's deliver services and how customers interact with their bank. Competition is no longer local and national institutions can reach into any market with acquisitions and technology. I believe board understanding of this changing, competitive environment is more challenging than the evolving regulatory environment.

Banking is a very dynamic business and successful banks require boards and management teams with a wide range of knowledge and skills to successfully address changing conditions. Many banks faced with increasing competition and higher costs due to increased regulatory requirements will elect to be acquired. Other bankers will see an opportunity to be an acquirer and grow. Bank boards will constantly be faced with very challenging strategic decisions that will impact shareholders, customers, employees and their communities.

The opportunity to serve as a member of a community bank board offers you a unique opportunity to provide your insight and personal skills to an institution that is an essential ingredient to the economic health of your community. If you are up to the task, the opportunity to see your bank, its employees, its shareholders and your community prosper will be your most significant personal reward.

Kick the Can . . . or Time to Go?

Perhaps it is time to 'plaque' a member of your board, or be 'plaqued' yourself.

Board membership is frequently an "ad hoc" process that only gets addressed when a vacancy occurs. Boards recognize the important role that management evaluations play in compensation programs and internal succession planning. However, the difficult topic of regular board member assessment is frequently ignored.

It is very difficult for board members to confront a fellow board member who is not fully contributing to your board's responsibilities. It is equally difficult for a board member to recognize when it is time to depart. It's easier for everyone to "kick the can down the road."

To be effective all boards must address board leadership, board size, required skill sets, board member performance and succession planning. Today's economic and regulatory environment requires your board to have the right people with the right skills to fulfill your board's duties.

Best practice requires your board to have independent leadership (either an independent chairman or lead director) and an independent board committee that's responsible for board governance. Your lead director should conduct an executive session with only outside directors after each board meeting and promptly discuss any significant items with the CEO. Your governance committee may provide a forum to openly evaluate the skill sets and performance of other board members, but any open self-assessment of committee members is problematic at best.

Given the complexity of today's board issues it is essential that a wide range of skills be represented and all board members actively contribute to your board's responsibilities. The American Association of Bank Directors recommends that every board conduct an annual self-assessment and have a confidential assessment done by an independent third party every three years. The results may not always be welcome but they will help enhance the quality of your board members.

Some boards use term limits or age limits as a mechanism to force rotation of board members. However, such programs impact both "quality" directors and "problem" directors and most likely permit the board to avoid addressing a need for change by "kicking the can" until the "problem" member hits the term/age limit.

Those of us who serve on nonprofit boards have most likely witnessed a board member getting "plaqued" — being honored and thanked for their service with a wall plaque or other memento as they exit the board. This is a gracious way many nonprofits give board members an honorable exit and rotate board members. Is it time to "plaque" a member of your board?

The most difficult situation may exist when a nice person just doesn't represent the right skill set or your board has an overabundance of duplicate skills (too many accountants or lawyers, etc.). Matching needed skill sets with a limited number of board seats requires an honest evaluation of individual skills and qualities — a very tough job for any board.

So, having read this brief article, it is time for your self-assessment. Do you still bring the right skills and work ethic to your boards or is it time for you to go?

As 2016 looms, your job as a bank director is . . .

Today's bank board agendas tend to be long on compliance and short on strategy. It's time for bank directors to shift focus from reacting to the swinging pendulum of ever-increasing regulatory compliance and work with management to initiate strategic leadership to better serve their bank's customers and communities.

The pendulum of regulatory and compliance requirements is continuing to swing and this focus on compliance with both new and old regulations tends to dominate time on board agendas. Regulatory frustration is pushing many boards to consider selling to another institution. Investment bankers are urging boards to sell as the best alternative to maximize shareholder value. However, selling your bank may not be the best outcome for your shareholders, your customers and your community.

Small business provides most job growth and our nation's 5,600 community banks provide essential financial services to small business in communities, large and small, across our nation. As I have stated in numerous articles, our nation's banking system provides the credit and liquidity required for economic growth. In simple terms, an engine won't run without oil and community banks provide the credit [oil] for economic growth in the communities we serve. Community banks have experienced no meaningful loan growth during the past seven years, a period when community bank boards have been reacting to increased regulation.

Your job as a bank director is to help guide your institution and leadership requires shifting your focus to strategic action, not just regulatory reaction. The following points should help guide your board agenda as we enter 2016.

• ***People:*** Most experts say selecting the right CEO is the board's most important job; I disagree. I believe your board's most important job is to select, recruit and retain board members with the right skill sets required to provide appropriate guidance and oversight for management.

The right board will select and retain the right CEO to lead your institution — poor boards lead to poor CEO selection.

Take the time as you enter next year to examine your board and make tough decisions if necessary; a bank director's job is too important to 'waste' a seat.

• **Strategy:** Your management and board are best positioned to identify the needs of your community and your bank must be positioned to service those needs. Effective strategy is not a 'large binder' on the shelf; it requires effective focus and action. As Yogi Berra famously observed: "If you don't know where you are going you might wind up someplace else."

For many banks lacking a clear strategy, that "someplace else" is down the road to sell the bank. Your job as a bank director is to make certain you have the right management team to design an effective strategy and deliver results.

• **Risk:** Inadequate board focus on the strategic risk associated with past real estate-related loan concentrations is now clearly apparent. Your board's challenge is to focus on strategic portfolio risk and not lose perspective by focusing on individual loan approval.

Board members are not loan officers and I continue to recommend that boards establish a risk committee to 1) evaluate investment, credit and funding policy, 2) review changes in asset concentrations and funding mix, 3) provide oversight over operating and technology risk, 4) monitor capital requirements and 5) not approve individual loans.

• **Compliance:** Regulatory compliance is a given; it's like breathing — you just do it. As a result, I suggest you consider establishing a separate board compliance committee to provide oversight over regulatory risk.
Boards have had a tendency to assign every new element of risk oversight to the audit committee and, as a result, audit committees are overburdened today. Establishing a board-level compliance committee would permit your audit committee to more appropriately focus on financial and accounting risk.

• **_Future Actions:_** Unforeseen events will impact the annual plans and budgets you establish to achieve your strategic objectives. Again, per Yogi Berra: "It's tough to make predictions, especially about the future."

The key to your bank's future success is having the right team and organizational structure to adapt your annual tactical actions so you achieve your strategic goals. Hopefully these thoughts help provide a few ideas for your next board agenda.

Directors Digest Articles

Directors Digest is a monthly online publication provided by the Western Independent Bankers Association [WIB].

This section includes quarterly articles that were published between 2011 and 2015 in my capacity as:

> Chairman, Chartwell Capital Ltd.
>
> Chairman, American Association of Bank Directors
>
> Chairman Emeritus, American Associate of Bank Directors

In addition to writing quarterly articles for 5 years I was also invited to make the following presentations at conferences hosted by the WIB.

> 2012 - Bank Directors Conference, San Francisco, CA
> "Lessons Learned"
>
> 2011 - Bank Directors Conference, San Diego, CA
> "Crisis Management"
>
> 2010 - Bank Directors Conference, San Francisco, CA
> "Dodd-Frank Act"
>
> 2009 - Bank Directors Conference, San Francisco, CA
> "Bank Director Liability"
>
> 2008 – Bank Directors Conference, San Francisco, CA
> "Bank Capital Planning"
>
> 2006 – Annual Bank Conference, Scottsdale, AZ
> "Executive Compensation"
>
> 2005 – Annual Bank Conference, Kauai, Hawaii
> "When Things Go Wrong"

Directors Digest – 1Q 2011

The Next Challenge?

A critical lesson learned from the past four years is the importance of both liquidity and asset/liability management. Each significant failure in 2008 was triggered by an inability to attract sufficient funding to "keep the doors open". Liquidity disappeared as a result of market fears related to asset quality and capital but the fatal flaw was funding.

Management has a responsibility to keep boards informed of management strategies to address market risks. Inadequate asset/liability management (ALCO) clearly contributed to the liquidity crisis at many institutions. It is essential that management address the full array of risks associated with ALCO. Five of the six regulatory CAMELS (Capital, Management, Earnings, Liquidity and Sensitivity) are directly related to ALCO management.

As a result, ALCO oversight is an essential part of board risk oversight. Interest rates are expected to increase from historically low levels as the economy recovers and interest rate risk is now receiving additional regulatory scrutiny. The following questions provide a starting point for understanding your bank's potential ALCO risks.

- Did your bank renegotiate loan pricing with "good customers" as rates declined to keep their business? Did your bank add "rate floors" to loan terms?

  Many banks incorporated "rate floors" to protect margins; however, such loans may not re-price promptly and margins will be squeezed as the cost of deposits increases. How much flexibility does your bank really have to increase loan pricing to offset an increase in the cost of deposits?

- Did your bank recognize securities gains in the past several years to enhance earnings and capital?

Unrealized gains and losses on securities don't impact regulatory capital ratios. As a result, it was necessary for many banks to sell securities and recognize gains to enhance capital ratios. Many banks also increased risk by extending maturities to enhance income when these funds were reinvested. An examination of year-end call reports indicates a growing number of banks now have unrealized securities losses.

This situation brings us full circle to liquidity risk and capital planning. To what extent will your bank's liquidity be compromised and capital ratios hurt if it becomes necessary to sell securities at a loss?

- Do your internal financial reports track your bank's tangible capital ratio?

Tangible capital received significant public and regulatory attention during the credit crisis but it is not currently a published regulatory capital ratio. Your bank's tangible capital will be negatively impacted as interest rates increase and the value of securities decreases. Do you know what impact an increase in interest rates will have on your tangible capital ratio?

- Has your board discussed the impact of potential changes in "Fair Value" accounting?

Fair Value accounting presents significant challenges for ALCO management and discussions should not be restricted to technical presentations at the audit committee. If required, Fair Value adjustments related to increasing interest rates would have a significant negative impact on bank capital ratios.

ALCO provides the tools for your management team to plan and navigate your bank's financial future. Growth, earnings sensitivity, capital and liquidity are all linked together and dependent upon one another. ALCO simulation models help management evaluate "what if" situations and to be better prepared to cope with changing conditions.

The board's role is to make certain your management team is systematically evaluating market risks and keeping your board informed of the potential consequences. However, your role is not to "step into the shoes" of management and attempt to "fine tune" ALCO activity – that's management's job.

Directors Digest – 2Q 2011

Governance Pendulum in Motion?

Congress, bank regulators, shareholders and governance 'experts' have all turned up the spotlight on board governance. Caution must be exercised so bank board members do not over-reach and step into the shoes of management – a situation that will compromise the board's essential role of management oversight.

Community bank board members are receiving no shortage of regulatory guidance and "expert" opinion concerning their roles. Every community bank board is a unique blend of experience and personalities and no single approach is best for every board. As a result, many recommendations may not reflect the reality of your bank's actual situation and could lead to unintended consequences.

The FDIC Office of Inspector General (OIG) prepares an assessment of individual bank failures. OIG assessments indicate many failed banks were dominated by strong individuals (the CEO, a board member or a shareholder) that were operating without adequate board oversight.

On the other hand, I have also witnessed situations where management was "delegating up" to the board – providing the board with a false sense of control and oversight. The following examples illustrate a few "red flags" for your board to consider.

First, don't confuse "control" with "leadership skills". The concept of a "split" role between the CEO and a board Chairman or Lead Director is now considered "best practice". I fully support the concept but defining this relationship is critical to effective board governance.

It's important to recognize the difference between individuals (in either role) that want to control the flow of board information and decision making with those individuals that exhibit the open leadership skills (such as described in my new book, *It Is What It Is*) required for effective management and oversight.

It's a serious "red flag" if your CEO ignores board policy or your bank's board chairman (or lead director) is engaging in day-to-day management decisions. Any attempt by any board member to control or suppress information and play politics to subvert management authority (hiring, termination, new loan, etc.) in "private" must be disclosed to the full board. Any such attempt to subvert the balance of authority calls for an executive session of your board to address the issue.

Second, don't let management delegate up! For example, your bank's loan approval policy can create a system that permits management to delegate credit decisions up to the board. It's a "red flag" if you hear the excuse "well, the board approved the (bad) loan". Board members have neither the time nor the credit skills to structure and approve loans and you should be on alert if management is delegating this task (or other management responsibilities) up to you.

Third, avoid stepping into a management vacuum. Recent asset quality problems have led to boards replacing senior executives at numerous institutions. In many cases regulatory consent orders require regulatory approval of new executive officers and this requirement delays recruitment during a very critical period.

Any CEO termination creates an obvious risk that board members or board committees step into the shoes of management. Pay careful attention if a board member assumes any temporary management role as they may find it difficult to resume an oversight role once the temporary management assignment has ended.

Fourth, don't be afraid to delegate. Your existing management team must be given the day-to-day authority to manage the bank – it should be obvious to every board member that day-to-day decisions cannot be made effectively by a board or board committee. Remember to "trust but verify" that management is following board policy.

Community bank board members are facing a difficult and evolving governance environment. In many banks the pendulum is swinging from passive reliance on the CEO to more active oversight by board members. Pendulums have a tendency to swing too far and boards and board members cannot provide their management oversight role if they are also engaged in day-to-day management decisions.

As board roles evolve it is important to consistently ask yourself "Does this action represent board oversight or are we stepping into the shoes of management"?

Directors Digest – 3Q 2011

Board Leadership

The recent financial crisis turned a spotlight on independent board leadership. Every board is comprised of individuals with different personalities, experience levels, and professional backgrounds; there is no "right answer" for every board. This article, based on our boardroom experience, provides a few thoughts and suggestions for your board to consider.

Lead Director or Chairman? We believe <u>function is far more important than title</u> and have witnessed effective board leadership by "independent" Lead Directors, Presiding Directors and Chairmen. Effective boards are always a work in progress and title is not as important as skillful board leadership to help your board adapt to changing circumstances.

Job Function? Your board's Lead Director has the potential to improve the effectiveness of your board or degrade it. It's essential that an <u>atmosphere of mutual respect</u> exist between your Lead Director, every member of your board and your bank's executive management team - especially between the Lead Director and the CEO.

The Lead Director's role may vary from bank to bank – based on the skills and personality of the individual. However, we believe an effective Lead Director:

- Presides (chair) at both board meetings and executive sessions
- Coordinates agendas with the CEO to address appropriate issues
- Encourages communication and facilitates questions during board meetings
- Leads executive sessions and encourages board feedback
- Focuses on quality and timeliness of information to the board
- Provides feedback from executive sessions to the CEO

Your Lead Director is not a member of bank management and, as discussed in our June article, must avoid stepping into the shoes of management. Your Lead Director, like every other board member, has just one vote. The essential role of independent oversight is lost if your Lead Director becomes involved in day-to-day management decisions.

Meeting Agendas? Your board meetings provide an excellent forum for directors to assess the depth of management without interfering in the CEO's day-to-day management responsibility. Senior officers should provide regular reports at every board meeting. The Lead Director should then excuse all non-board members as a group when all management reports are completed so the board and CEO can discuss bank business in private.

At the conclusion of your board's regular business meetings, the CEO and board secretary should be excused so outside board members can discuss bank business privately in "executive session".

Executive Sessions? We believe regular executive sessions at the end of every board meeting are in everyone's best interest. However, we recognize that many CEOs and board members don't think a "regular" executive session is necessary.

CEOs must recognize that directors will discuss bank business with one another informally (at social events, their clubs, etc.) if a regular time and location for private discussion is not provided. Regular executive sessions help both the CEO and board members avoid "lobbying" by individual directors outside the boardroom. The executive session is the proper time and place for the Lead Director to ask each director if they have anything they wish to discuss.

It is important for outside directors to limit discussion to important policy topics. The executive session is not a forum for petty issues or personal grievances. The executive session is not an excuse for the board to become involved in day-to-day management issues. It is essential that directors avoid unintended conflict and respect the roles of the CEO and bank management.

It's also important for board members to remember the boardroom is a "fish bowl", everyone knows you are in executive session. For this reason, a regular executive session at the end of every board meeting becomes "routine", not "special". Board members have a responsibility to allow adequate time for board business and not "rush out" at the end of board meetings to attend other matters.

Board members need to be sensitive to the potential "unintended consequences" of a long executive session, open the door when business is done, this is not the time or place to have a prolonged discussion about a sporting event.

The <u>Lead Director must always brief the CEO immediately after the executive session</u> on the topics discussed during your meeting. This follow-up is essential to maintaining positive CEO-board relations and needs to occur even if no topic of substance was discussed.

This brief article shares a few of my thoughts concerning "best practice" for board leadership. In my view "best practice" is best based on the collective experience of actual board members (not non-board member experts), and I welcome your feedback.

Directors Digest – 4Q 2011

Piñatas & Tsunamis

"Banks" and "bankers" are today's political piñata and everyone feels entitled to take a swipe. As a result, the Dodd-Frank Act represents an upcoming Tsunami of increased bank regulation. As bank directors we have an opportunity and an obligation to 'step back' and help guide our institutions through this increasingly treacherous political and regulatory landscape.

It's also important to recognize that bank regulators face an overwhelming task of interpreting Dodd-Frank, writing over 300 new regulations and designing the required enforcement procedures. Bank regulators are the referees designated by Congress to enforce Dodd-Frank.

Much of Dodd-Frank is "principles" based and many of these principles represent sound business practice especially in the areas of incentive compensation and customer pricing. As board members we have a unique opportunity to put ourselves in the shoes of our shareholders and our customers.

The "rules" required by Dodd-Frank's Section 956 (incentive compensation) apply to banks over $1 billion; however, the "principles" apply to every bank. As a result, community banks must also avoid implementing incentive plans that may lead (in the eyes of your examiner) to unsafe and unsound practices. Wall Street compensation practices created the spotlight but volume based incentive programs to encourage growth without appropriate risk controls existed at community banks.

In addition community bank directors are frequently expected to introduce new business to their bank. Its important to recognize that not all officer incentives are monetary and such introductions may encourage your credit officers to approve marginal credits to please a board member.

Dodd-Frank's requirement for boards to review all incentive programs is the result of poor programs throughout our industry. Implementing incentive programs to insure that today's short-term results also result in solid long-term results will better align incentive compensation with shareholder interest and regulatory requirements.

Dodd-Frank's focus on consumer pricing also represents an opportunity to better understand how our customers view our products and services. Put yourself in the shoes of your customers – would you consider the price structure of your bank's products and services to be "fair" to your mother or child?

A prime example was the introduction of "high to low" check processing combined with an increase in overdraft fees - a practice that was destined to attract the attention of consumer activists, their legal teams and finally Congress.

Poor practice in the eyes of the public and the knee-jerk reaction by Congress produced Dodd-Frank; 2,300 pages of legislation that failed to address government mortgage policy at the GSEs and created the new Consumer Financial Protection Bureau (CFPB) the new "cop on the beat" to protect your bank's bank customers. Dodd-Frank penalizes every bank – guilty or not. The risk today is that legislative principles become regulatory rules that become an unsupportable burden for all community banks.

Bankers at several recent conferences complained privately that presentations by bank regulators did not provide enough clarity on the upcoming tsunami of new "guidance" for community banks. Be careful what you wish for – specificity requires detailed rules that will limit the flexibility that "principles" based guidance provides your bank. One size does not fit all and community banks have been granted an opportunity to exercise sound judgment rather than be forced to just "check another box".

Bank regulatory agencies have a monumental training job ahead to insure appropriate examination procedures and it is not realistic to assume every examiner will exercise good judgment. On the other hand, bank examiners view conditions and practices at other banks throughout your market area and have unique market perspective. Many observations to your board may be based on knowledge they cannot disclose.

As board members you will gain valuable perspective if you ask questions and listen to bank regulators in addition to your regular meetings with bank management. Exercise "good faith" efforts to follow the "principles" in Dodd-Frank and consider having management "preview" selected programs with your regulators prior to introduction.

Share your experience with Dodd-Frank enforcement with your banking associations. Dodd-Frank is dumping a monumental workload on bank examiners, bank management and bank directors. We are all playing this new game with revised rules together and arguing with a referee seldom produces the desired result.

Directors Digest – 1Q 2012

Bank Consolidation to Remain Elusive

Each of the last several years has opened with ever-hopeful investment bankers predicting of a new wave of bank acquisition activity among community banks. Predictions of significant acquisition activity have proved to be overly optimistic in past years but today's question remains: "Will 2012 mark the beginning of community bank consolidation?" We remain skeptical for the following reasons.

• Many community bankers remain overly optimistic about acquisition pricing. The days of cash transactions with significant premiums to book value are not returning in the foreseeable future.

• Potential acquirors remain very concerned about asset quality – buyers don't want to acquire another bank's problems.

• Bank regulators continue to be focused on equity capital and will be very reluctant to approve transactions that reduce regulatory capital ratios.

There is no question that smaller community banks are facing a multitude of financial and management challenges including modest asset growth (if any), compressed margins and the increased cost of compliance. However, the most significant challenge may well be the difficulty of attracting quality people to smaller institutions in an industry that is clearly out of favor with both Congress and the public. The opportunity to exit this hostile environment with a cash premium would be hard to resist for many community bankers.

On the other hand the financial challenge for an acquiror is to target institutions big enough to impact financial performance (earnings per share) but small enough to consolidate without problems. A brief description of the hurdles faced by potential acquirors will help put the situation in perspective.

The days of leveraged cash acquisitions funded by TruPS are history. Future acquisition activity will need to be funded with equity – the issuance of shares.

Intangible assets (goodwill) created by purchase accounting reduce regulatory capital and provide a roadblock to the payment of any significant premium. The financial impact of booking acquired loans at a discount has come as a surprise to many potential acquirors. Sadly the impact of regulatory accounting rather than economics will drive many future transactions.

Potential sellers generally desire liquidity (cash or listed shares) and may not even consider a combination that does not offer at least some liquidity. Today's environment restricts acquisitions to a few very well capitalized institutions and those 'public' institutions with access to capital at attractive multiples.

There are over 5,000 community banks with under $500 million in assets. The most likely potential acquirors are among the 420 institutions included in the Community Bank Index (ABAQ). However, not all of these 420 NASDAQ listed banks have sufficient earnings or capital to become acquirors. The net result is too few potential acquirors positioned to engage in significant consolidation of smaller community banks.

We do expect to see an increase in community bank consolidation but expect many transactions to be carefully structured to protect the buyer. For example, branch transactions provide selling banks an opportunity to become more efficient and profitable and buyers can also benefit with expanded markets and new customers. Branch acquisitions with the assumption of deposits and the purchase of only performing assets help buyers avoid many liabilities associated with whole bank acquisitions.

We also expect to see more unique 'whole-bank' transactions structured similar to branch transactions such as the recent acquisition of First Independent Bank announced by Sterling Financial. Potential acquirors are clearly in the drivers seat today.

We have one final caution for both potential buyers and sellers. Don't start discussions if you are not fully prepared to engage in mutual due-diligence that will be even more detailed than a regulatory exam. You both have only one opportunity to get it right and avoid post transaction surprises.

Our recent advice to a community-banking client to reject a public tender offer by a larger institution at a significant market premium was validated when the potential acquiror subsequently reported significant asset quality problems.

In conclusion, we advise community bank CEOs and their boards to focus on managing their institution as if they will own it forever – planning to sell is not a plan. The only time to consider a sale today is when a qualified buyer expresses interest in your institution – and proceed with caution.

Directors Digest – 2Q 2012

Bank Director Burdens & Risks

Every bank director knows that "Your bank's board needs to (insert topic)" are words being expressed with increasing frequency by bank examiners.

The Bank Director Regulatory Burden Report, authored by David Baris and recently published by the American Association of Bank Directors, has identified over 800 legislative and regulatory provisions that have accumulated over many decades that impact the responsibilities of bank directors!

The Dodd-Frank Act is only the most recent legislative action that increases the burden placed on directors of financial institutions and the 800+ provisions in the AABD Report do not include new additions required by Dodd-Frank. The aggregate impact of all federal legislation, regulation and regulatory "guidance" is an ever- increasing tsunami of bank regulation impacting bank directors.

The 177-page AABD Report summarizes current regulatory requirements, grouped by regulatory agency. Regulatory "guidance" is included as board members know that examiners apply "guidance" no differently than a regulation – including "guidance" that is managerial in nature. However, the role of any board is oversight, not day-to-day management, and actions that divert the attention of your bank's board away from your oversight role is a mistake.

It is evident that no one - not Congress and not the federal banking agencies – is evaluating the aggregate effect government actions are having on the duties and responsibilities of bank directors. This new AABD Report is the result of an extensive review of federal legislation, federal bank regulations, and federal banking agency guidance to identify existing provisions that can and do overwhelm bank directors.

When you were invited to serve on the board of your local bank you knew the President and many of the people on the board. You considered the bank to be an important contributor to growth in your community and it was an honor to be offered a place on the board of directors. Personal liability was probably not foremost in your mind when you accepted.

As a bank board member you routinely make decisions and vote on matters based on your good faith business judgment. You're not thinking about how someone from one of the banking agencies might judge your actions after the fact.

This ever-increasing regulatory burden is a significant distraction from board time necessary for risk oversight and other essential board responsibilities. The increasing threat of regulatory and personal liability is forcing bank boards to become "compliance" boards where attention must be focused on satisfying laws, regulations, and regulatory guidance that pertain to duties that are the function of day-to-day management.

Any review of the regulatory provisions identified in the AABD Report needs to focus on the appropriate role of board oversight. Many regulatory provisions, if not carefully considered, can lead boards to the mistaken conclusion they need to "step into the shoes of management'. Doing so is a serious error that can substantially increase your potential liability as a bank director.

The AABD is currently analyzing FDIC complaints filed against directors of failed banks during the past three years. Initial analysis clearly indicates that, among other actions, bank directors should reconsider their role in the direct approval of loans. Boards should reexamine the role of the director's loan committee and ask if your board is permitting bank management to "delegate up" and shift responsibility and liability up to you as board members.

I believe that bank boards can respond and will manage the burdens and risks to directors through a thoughtful corporate governance process that includes not just controlling risks to the institution but also risks to directors. Periodic assessments of how your board conducts its business should also include evaluations of whether the decisions you are making are made in a way that will also protect you personally if questioned years after decisions are made.

I can only hope that this important AABD Report leads to a constructive dialog with bank regulators and does not discourage talented individuals from joining or remaining on bank boards.

Directors Digest – 3Q 2012

Time for Change?

AABD's Bank Director Regulatory Burden Report identifies over 800 legislative and regulatory provisions that have accumulated over many decades that impact the responsibilities of bank directors!

It is evident that no one – not Congress and not the federal banking agencies – is evaluating the aggregate effect government actions are having on the duties and responsibilities of bank directors.

This growing regulatory burden is a significant distraction from board time necessary for risk oversight and other essential board responsibilities. Ever-increasing regulatory liability is forcing bank boards to become "compliance" boards where attention is focused on satisfying laws, regulations, and regulatory guidance pertaining to duties that are properly the function of day-to-day management.

Bank directors can choose one of three basic routes to navigate today's ever-increasing regulatory burden: resign, play "check the box" or face the challenge. This article offers a few suggestions to those board members who elect to face the challenge.

1. *Time management is our first challenge as board members*

How do we allocate sufficient board time to meet our growing compliance duties and still provide appropriate strategic guidance and risk oversight? One approach you might consider is scheduling specific agendas for individual board meetings rather than following the same routine agenda for every board meeting. For example, devote one meeting each quarter to focus on financial matters, one meeting for compliance matters and a third meeting for a special topic such as strategic planning, risk oversight, a "deep dive" into major business units or any specific topic that is of current importance.

2. *Utilize your board committees*

Delegate and allocate board responsibilities. Review and modify board committee charters (your committee's job description) if necessary to meet today's requirements. Do you have the right committees with the right leadership and membership to meet today's requirements for governance, compensation, audit and risk oversight?

3. *Establish a separate board risk committee to focus on your bank's overall risk appetite and policy limits for credit, asset/liability and operational risks*

A separate risk committee permits your audit committee to focus on oversight of financial reporting, internal controls and regulatory compliance. I believe this approach provides a better allocation of board member time with improved focus on upcoming risk (looking out the windshield) and retains your audit committee's oversight of operations and compliance. Your risk (or governance) committee should also identify "red flags" representing risks of potential personal liability.

4. *Work with your bank's CEO to reassess all board reports*

Is it time to eliminate, simplify, expand or add individual reports? We all know that many board reports have a tendency to grow over time and new reports must be added to meet new regulatory requirements. The net result becomes report overload with diminished focus on the essential elements of board oversight.

5. *Stop approving loans!*

Don't let management delegate credit decisions up to the board. Board members have neither the time nor the credit skills to structure and approve loans and you should be on alert if management is delegating this task (or other management responsibilities) to you. Your board should focus on oversight and approval of credit policy (loan limits, types, concentrations, etc.) that include all credit exposures (loans, investments, counterparties, etc). Credit analysis and individual loan approval is a management responsibility and it's a "red flag" if you hear the excuse "well, the board approved the (bad) loan".

6. *Today's ever-changing economic and regulatory environment requires every board to reassess board membership*

Do you have the right people on your board with the right skills to address today's challenges? We all know it's very tough to face a board member that is no longer making the required contribution. An annual assessment of board member performance is essential and AABD recommends an independent third-party assessment be undertaken every three years.

7. *Board education is a continuous process that can be achieved from a wide variety of sources*

Look to the Internet (WIB.org & AABD.org), online publications (this WIB Directors Digest), email (AABD Alert), traditional publications, webinars and conferences. Your best source of new ideas may well be other directors you meet at conferences. Face-to-face networking remains a very valuable source of new ideas. Finally, I want to extend my invitation to attend the 2012 Annual Directors Conference hosted by WIB and AABD on November 8-10 in San Francisco. Our conference, designed by directors for directors, offers both an excellent program and a valuable venue for networking with other bank directors.

Just a few points for your consideration – as always, I welcome your feedback.

Directors Digest – 4Q 2012

It's That Time of Year – Again

It's time for your bank's board to evaluate the performance and pay of your CEO, evaluate the performance of your board and its committees and look in the mirror and also evaluate your own performance. Does your bank have the right management team combined with the right mix of board talent to guide your institution in today's economic and regulatory environment?

Shareholder expectations and regulatory requirements for the evaluation of the performance and pay of your chief executive officer and other members of your executive team continue to evolve. The guiding principles for executive incentive compensation programs (both stock and cash) require that payments be linked to sustained performance over time.

Your board's most significant compensation challenge today is the determination of realistic performance expectations, not plan design. The current economic environment combined with higher regulatory capital requirements impacts typical performance benchmarks such as return on shareholder equity. Your board's challenge this year is to focus on both the benchmarks used to measure performance and to determine the level of long-term performance that represents an acceptable target for incentive compensation payments.

As always, I caution boards to remember that regulatory peer group performance is an "average" and suggest that, in most circumstances, incentive payouts linked to average performance might be compared to rewarding your children for receiving a "C" in school. However, in this environment, a target linked to improving year-to- year results might well represent a reasonable performance plan. Setting realistic long-term performance targets is a challenging job in today's economic and regulatory environment.

Many organizations, including the American Association of Bank Directors, offer a variety of tools for the internal evaluation of your board's performance. Utilizing a simple questionnaire that provides "feel good" results is a waste of time – worthwhile board evaluations are hard work. It's not easy to evaluate your board's performance or for you to pass judgment on the quality of other board members.

Board assessments provide your board with the opportunity to take early intervention when potential board governance or board membership issues develop. The AABD recommends a 360° assessment of board governance including [a] a self-assessment by each board member, [b] a group assessment by each board member and [c] an assessment of board governance by executive management. It's generally best if these assessments remain confidential and are returned to a third party such as outside counsel or a board advisor.

Finally, take the time to look in the mirror and accurately evaluate your own performance. The increased regulatory burden has also increased your individual responsibilities and the potential liability of your entire board. Are you doing your job?

Your board and committee charters are your "job description" and provide the roadmap for both group and individual evaluations. But performance is more than a "check the box" activity on a questionnaire – you need to ask yourself if you and your board have the right structure and the right people to do the job.

Increased regulatory expectations (special AABD reports available) combined with today's economic climate are forcing many banks to re-evaluate their business plans and performance expectations. Strategic discussions at many community banks have shifted from growth to finding an exit strategy and individual directors are questioning the wisdom of their continued bank board service.

Today's economic challenges and regulatory burden may have increased but its also important for bank directors to remember that our nation's banking system provides the necessary credit and liquidity for private business to grow and our nation to prosper. Today's regulatory environment may be tossing 'sand in the gears' but your bank still serves as the oil in the economic engine of your community.

My advice to the board and executive management of any community bank is to "manage your institution as if you will own it forever" and focus on those actions you can take to serve your customers and prosper with your community. Meaningful executive and board evaluations help insure that your institution has the right people on both the board and in management to guide the future success your bank.

Directors Digest - 1Q 2013

Bank M&A: Buy, Sell or Hold?

This year, like each of the past several years, has started with predictions of renewed bank merger and acquisition (M&A) activity. Of course, many such predictions originate with investment bankers having a vested interest in increased activity. Predictions for increased M&A activity at the community bank level are based on a variety of factors: low interest rates; declining margins; modest loan demand (at best); increased competition from larger banks; and most important, increased regulatory requirements and costs. It's easy to paint a gloomy picture for community banking.

Senior bank regulators have recently stressed the importance of community banking to local communities. However, many bankers question the sincerity of such public statements given the increased regulatory cost and compliance risk of doing business as a community bank. The reluctance of the FDIC to approve new charters also brings into question its commitment to community banking.

My presentation at the American Bankers M&A Conference in New York last February questioned any significant increase in 2012 bank M&A activity. I was half- right; although the number of reported transactions increased from 163 to 227, the total value of transactions actually declined from $17 billion to $14 billion.

So – what's really happening?

Many community bankers have received dinner invitations from investment bankers who would not return their phone call a few years ago. M&A focus has shifted from regional banks to smaller community banks; however, smaller transactions at lower prices also places pressure on investment bank M&A fee income. As a result, M&A advisory firms are also consolidating as evidenced by the recently completed acquisition of Keefe, Bruyette & Woods, Inc. by Stifel Financial Corp.

The limited number of potential buyers with a premium stock price multiple must exercise pricing discipline if they are to maintain their acquisition advantage. Several post-acquisition studies indicate many bank combinations only increase size (and CEO compensation) but do not enhance shareholder value. Successful acquisition strategies are built utilizing premium stock multiples based on disciplined pricing and earnings per share growth that enhances shareholder value.

It's also important for potential sellers to carefully evaluate the potential long-term value of any shares to be received in a proposed transaction. Beware the deal that's "too good to be true". For example, several years ago, we successfully advised a client to reject a hostile exchange offer "valued" at $9 per share at a time when their institution's stock price was $4.50 per share. Today, the shares from that $9 exchange offer would be worth less than $1 and the client's stock price exceeds $9 as an independent bank. It's essential that sellers also do their homework (with qualified financial and legal advisors)!

It's very difficult, if not impossible, to make the numbers work for most potential M&A transactions between community banks of similar size. I continue to predict that a significant number of community banks with a desire to sell will be "orphans" with no choice but to enhance future value as an independent bank. Planning to sell is not a plan.

So – if planning to sell is not a plan – then what? My advice for decades has been, "Manage your bank as if you will own it forever – if you don't you most likely will." Successful strategic buyers want to acquire high quality banks in markets that offer the opportunity for future growth. It makes no difference if you want to buy, sell or remain independent – focus on building a solid institution for the long term.

Successful community bankers have identified survival and growth strategies in past difficult periods – a few of us remember 1973-74, 1979-81 and 1989-91. Well- managed institutions emerged stronger, not weaker, after each of these troubled periods.

I continue to believe there is an important role for well-managed community banks. Community banks can and do offer more personalized service than the large regional or national banks. Technology provided by quality service providers help level the playing field for community banks. Community banks can better manage the regulatory and compliance burden if they target products and services to their community and don't attempt to be all things to all people.

It's a very tough time but both bank directors and executive management have an obligation to their bank's shareholders to build a solid institution and enhance shareholder value. It won't be easy in today's environment but you really have no choice.

Director's Digest - 2Q 2013

To Be or Not To Be...Chairman

The publicity surrounding the chairmanship of JP Morgan has focused attention on the evolving role of independent board leadership. In my view, the focus on title rather than function is misplaced.

The American Association of Bank Directors recently published a special report listing over 800 laws, regulations and regulatory guidance that impact board members. The responsibilities of independent non-management board members at all banks continues to increase and it is important that your board consider all essential issues before a regulatory exam and have a regular process for independent board members to address any concerns with your CEO.

Every board has a unique mix of people and talent and, as a result, a simple cookie-cutter separation of chairman and CEO titles may not be the best answer for every financial institution. In any event, your board leader must be an individual who can stay strategic and maneuver through difficult issues and subjects dispassionately. This article addresses a couple of alternatives for the boards of any bank, including non-publicly traded community banks, to consider.

Split the Titles: Chief Executive with an Independent Chairman:

This is the approach that receives the most outside expert attention. The concept is simple; an independent non-executive chairman determines the board agenda, conducts all board meetings and leads an executive session of all independent board members (without the CEO). However, I have two primary concerns with this approach.

First, your board may find it difficult to replace someone designated with such a lofty title without a forcing a resignation. Just because a director doesn't continue as chairman doesn't mean that individual would not be a very valuable and experienced board member.

Also, when such an independent non-executive chairman has office space at the bank then I question if that individual truly serves as an independent non-executive.

Lead Director:

A number of boards designate a lead director to conduct executive sessions of all independent board members without the chairman/CEO in the boardroom. The lead director is then charged with discussing all issues (good and bad) raised during this private executive session in a follow- up meeting with the chairman/CEO.

This approach provides all independent directors with an opportunity for confidential discussions with one another and a regular process for the lead director to address any concerns with the chairman/CEO. However, as chairman, the CEO continues to conduct board meetings.

Lead Director as Board Leader:

A modified approach is to assign your lead director with the responsibility to [a] mutually determine the agenda for each board meeting with the chairman/CEO, [b] actually conduct (chair) each board meeting, [c] conduct the executive session with all independent directors and [d] privately discuss all issues raised during the executive session with the chairman/CEO.

I believe the selection of a lead director who in fact assumes the responsibilities of board meeting leadership may offer the best approach for internal independent board governance for many financial institutions without a lofty title that may make it difficult to replace or rotate board leadership. The job description of the lead director is far more important than the title.

Executive Sessions:

Finally, the most important role of the independent board leader (chairman or lead director) is to conduct an executive session with all independent board members after every board meeting without any members of management. In addition, a dominant non-management shareholder serving as a board member might not be considered to be independent. In such circumstances, your board might consider holding its executive sessions with only your independent board members.

In any event, I believe it is essential for the executive session leader to go around the table and ask each director at every meeting if there is anything they want to share with the other board members. This is the forum for open discussion and one-on-one discussion of individual viewpoints outside the boardroom should be discouraged.

All bank board members have unique legal and regulatory responsibilities that increase their individual liability. As a result, non-management board members are well served by designating a leader to conduct regular private executive sessions to insure their interests are appropriately considered.

Directors Digest - 3Q 2013

Risk Oversight & Your Bank's Board

Is your board prepared to discuss risk oversight with your bank's regulators in your next exit meeting? What will bank regulators expect your board to be doing in your role of risk oversight?

These questions do not have concise answers today. Regulatory guidelines are evolving and focused on systemically important financial institutions. However, experience has taught community bank directors that regulatory expectations for large financial institutions tend to trickle down.

On July 17 the Financial Stability Board (FSB) published *Principles for an Effective Risk Appetite Framework (RAF)*. The FSB Principles "set out key elements for: (i) an effective risk appetite framework, (ii) an effective risk appetite statement, (iii) risk limits, and (iv) *define the roles and responsibilities of the board of directors and senior management.*"

Definitions often differ across regulatory jurisdictions and the FSB Principles aim to establish common nomenclature to "help facilitate a common understand between regulators and (banks)." **Risk Appetite Framework (RAF)** The FSB indicates that an appropriate RAF should define your bank's risk capacity, risk appetite, risk limits and risk profile.

Some examples:

• Your bank's legal lending limit might be $20 million but your internal policy limit is $10 million

• Regulatory guidelines for loan concentrations may exceed your internal limitations, and/or

• Your board may have established bond portfolio duration limitations to limit interest rate risk.

All such policy limits must be considered as a whole to understand your bank's existing risk profile.

Risk Committee? FSB Principles do not prescribe how your board should provide oversight of bank strategy, your business plan and the models and systems to measure and aggregate risks.

Many banks have established board Risk Committees. I believe the role for such committees must be carefully integrated with the role of the full board and other committees such as audit. The overlay of a new Risk Committee within your existing board and committee structure may be counterproductive.

The American Association of Bank Directors (AABD) recommends that board members not approve individual loans (except Reg. O). Board members should focus on such issues as credit policy, loan concentrations, interest rate risk, operational risk, compliance risk and regulatory risk. The work related to credit and interest rate risk oversight is an appropriate assignment for a board risk committee and provides an opportunity to replace existing board committees such as loan and investment.

The distinction of duties between the Risk Committee and the Audit Committee can be described as the following:

The **Risk Committee's** job is to focus on setting and monitoring polices and limits outlined by the FSB Principles – looking out the windshield and providing guidance to keep your bank out of the ditch.

The job of the **Audit Committee** is to insure that management is in compliance with external regulatory requirements and is operating within the policies and limits established by the Risk Committee. Audit Committees are already overburdened and a Risk Committee is complimentary, not an overlap with Audit Committee responsibilities. Some degree of shared committee membership may help avoid overlap and prevent gaps.

Many specialized consulting firms are in the process of broadening their services to include enterprise risk management (ERM). When seeking outside guidance it is important for your new Risk Committee to maintain perspective and not just adopt a cookie-cutter ERM program designed to enhance fee income for a consulting firm.

FSB Principles list 12 responsibilities for the board of directors, which may be assigned to your Risk Committee. These responsibilities include:

• Approve the firm's RAF, developed in collaboration with the CEO, CRO and CFO.

• Hold the CEO and other senior management accountable for the integrity of the RAF.

• Regularly review and monitor actual versus approved risk limits.

• Obtain an independent assessment (through internal assessors, third parties or both) of the design and effectiveness of the RAF.

Over time, I expect these responsibilities to become part of all regulatory exams, including community banks. They represent best practice today and I recommend they be reviewed and incorporated by your board in advance of regulatory requirements.

Directors Digest - 4Q 2013

Regulatory Fatigue

Numerous articles, many written by investment bankers, describe the regulatory hurdles facing community banks and conclude that consolidation is the only rational economic outcome. Community bankers require significant stamina to weather the growing onslaught of "trickle down" regulation related to Dodd-Frank and regulatory fatigue is frequently cited as a key contributor to a board's decision to sell.

Historical data published by the FDIC appears to contradict the proposition that smaller community banks cannot compete nor generate sufficient returns to justify continued independence. FDIC data in the following table illustrates that smaller community banks not only weathered the recession better than larger institutions but also continue to operate profitably.

However, larger institutions now appear to be absorbing increased regulatory costs better than smaller institutions. Most important, the time required by both bank management and bank boards to manage this increased regulatory burden presents a significant diversion of focus from providing essential financial services to customers.

In October the Federal Reserve and the Conference of State Bank Supervisors (CSBS) hosted "Community Banking in the 21st Century." It's no surprise to bankers that presentations at the conference indicated community banks are under siege from increased regulation. As bankers, we can only hope that increased regulatory awareness actually results in positive regulatory change.

However, in my view, the most significant hurdle we face today is not economic or regulatory – it's the fact that "banks" have become a media, political and legal piñata – everybody feels entitled to take a (frequently inaccurate) swipe. As a result, the Gallup Survey reported the public's confidence in their bank (including community banks) had fallen to a record low of 21 percent in 2012.

Our nation's banking system provides the lubricating oil for our nation's economy. Community banks serve an essential role in the economic health of their communities. Employment data indicates that most of our nation's new jobs are related to hiring by small business – the primary business customers of community banks.

The banking industry requires qualified people to deliver essential financial services and, in my view, our greatest long-term risk will be the reluctance of quality people to join such an unpopular industry. Respect for banks and bankers must be restored to attract the new people required for management and board succession to support future economic growth.

Return on Equity	2008	2009	2010	2011	2012
$100 to $300M	3.40%	0.04%	2.47%	5.48%	7.75%
$300 to $500M	2.00%	-1.05%	3.20%	5.81%	8.29%
$500M to $1B	2.47%	-2.80%	2.27%	5.65%	8.23%
$1B to $10B	-2.06%	-4.12%	1.16%	7.22%	10.08%

In this environment it's no surprise that under-appreciated and over-regulated community bankers and their boards are suffering from fatigue. As a result, it's also no surprise that acquisition discussion is on many board agendas. The perfect size for any business (banks included) always seems to be bigger, no matter what size the business. The goal of any business is to grow and prosper.

Acquisition by a larger institution can offer the boards of smaller community banks an exit from this very unpleasant environment. However, the wave of bank mergers projected by many (hopeful) investment bankers has not materialized to date.

There are many hurdles to a successful acquisition; purchase accounting, regulatory requirements, price expectations, social issues, etc. Most quality buyers have a wide choice of markets and institutions. Potential sellers may discover few interested buyers and face a disappointing lack of interest.

However, as in the past, successful community bankers will look past these challenges and work to invigorate economic growth within their communities. Local and regional economic growth will need to be grass roots in nature given the disappointing failure of leadership being displayed by our nation's elected officials.

For decades, I have advised bankers to "manage your institution as if you will own it forever – if you don't you just might." Quality buyers tend to target quality institutions and the time to consider a sale is when things are going very well – not the result of management and board fatigue.

I believe many community banks will remain independent and provide the leadership necessary for their communities to successfully overcome today's economic challenges. The community bank conference hosted by the Federal Reserve and CSBS suggests that even our regulators understand that community banks play an essential role in our economy.

Directors Digest - 1Q 2014

Risk Oversight and Board Responsibilities

On January 10, 2014, the OCC published proposed enforceable guidelines for the establishment and oversight of risk policy at national banks and federal savings associations with $50 billion of consolidated assets. However, it's important to note, the OCC reserves the right to apply the Guidelines to national banks and federal savings associations with less than $50 billion assets if they present "heightened risks". It is also possible that bank examiners from any agency could informally apply the Guidelines to community banks as best practice. As a result, I personally believe the OCC's proposal deserves the attention of all bank directors.

First, the proposed guidelines provide a distinction between the roles of front-line management, executive management and the board of directors. This distinction is a welcome departure from the historic practice of stating, "management and the board" [with little or no distinction].

This past regulatory failure to clearly separate the roles of day-to-day management and independent director oversight has been a major contributor to the existing 800+ rules and regulations identified by the American Association of Bank Directors (AABD) in the "Bank Director Regulatory Burden Report".

However, in my opinion, this clarification of roles actually offers little comfort to board members, as the proposed guidelines are part of the OCC's "Heightened Expectations" for governance. In my experience, many rules, regulations and regulatory orders are less about constructive guidance and more about whom to blame (board members) if and when things go wrong. I expect such "heightened regulatory expectations" will also heighten the personal liability for individual bank directors expected to ensure that an effective risk governance framework is established.

Second, the (job) descriptions contained in the proposed guidelines related to day-to-day risk management and board oversight provide a framework that should prove informative to banks of all sizes.

Third, it's actually refreshing to see a relatively short publication (79 pages) related to a bank regulatory proposal (the final Volcker Rule was 1,077 pages). The actual guidelines are about 20 pages long and the 336 words comprising the "Standards for Board of Directors" succinctly address each of the following key issues that are relevant to all bank directors:

• Ensure an effective risk governance framework

• Provide active oversight of management

• Exercise independent judgment

• Provide ongoing training to independent directors

• Self-assessments

The "heightened expectations" described in the full proposal are clearly designed for large institutions. However, I believe the basic elements described provide a good checklist for directors at all institutions.

The scope of the proposed risk governance framework covers credit risk, interest rate risk, liquidity risk, price risk, operational risk, compliance risk, strategic risk and reputation risk. Based on my experience, most community banks are already addressing these elements.

Defining and "ensuring" an effective risk governance framework is the most difficult step for both management and the board of directors to implement in a community bank. Linking the various elements together while maintaining an appropriate separation of duties and independence is a difficult task for community banks with limited financial and human resources. In any event, an appropriate tone at the top is critical to establishing a sound risk management culture.

Your bank's strategic plan is the starting point for defining the level of risk (Risk Appetite) that your management and the board are willing to undertake to achieve your financial objectives. For example, your plan's definitions of target loan types, credit criteria, size limits, geographic exposure and concentration limits will help set your bank's credit risk parameters.

As you know, banking is the art of managing risk, not eliminating risk. People at all levels of your organization engage in risky activity every day – cashing checks, taking deposits (AML risk), making loans, approving loans, making investments, processing customer information, etc.

An organizational structure that provides your bank with independent credit and risk management personnel combined with an independent internal audit function will help provide an appropriate "trust but verify" structure that helps prevent both management and board surprises.

As a result, talent management, including training and compensation plans at all levels, is essential for internal risk management. My assignments during the financial crisis uncovered incentive compensation plans that were established without an appropriate "check and balance" contributed to excessive risk, excessive losses and regulatory orders. For example, loan officer incentive plans based on volume require a system of independent credit approval, including a potential veto by credit officers to ensure that loan officers don't overrule credit officers.

Furthermore, a reminder to board members that you should avoid stepping into the shoes of management and don't personally approve loans. Board members are not credit officers and board approval of loans permits management to delegate credit risk up to you and significantly increase your personal liability. It's essential that directors serve in an oversight role, as described by the OCC, and avoid accepting needless additional personal liability.

The AABD is planning to submit comments to the OCC on the proposed guidelines and I recommend both executive management and board members read and provide feedback on these official AABD comments when published.

I believe community bank directors face a growing risk of trickle-down regulation and you ignore increasing regulatory risk at your own personal peril. I find it a curious oversight that the OCC did not more clearly specify regulatory risk as a significant element in board risk oversight.

Directors Digest - 2Q 2014

Today's Top Board Expectations

During the past year, I participated on several programs with bank regulators discussing regulatory expectations for community bank directors. Regulatory expectations and regulator concerns vary somewhat between the banking agencies and the following topics and viewpoints represent my interpretation of these panel discussions.

Job Description: We all know that bank regulators have high expectations for bank directors. Bank regulations place burdens on bank directors that exceed the duties for directors of non-financial institutions and the Bank Director Regulatory Burden Report published by the AABD identified over 800 rules and regulations that impact bank directors.

As a result, your starting point to meet these higher expectations is having the appropriate mix of individual skills on your bank's board, the selection of quality management [People You Trust] and the establishment of strong governance and oversight systems [Verify].

Talent: The banking industry has received a 'black eye' over the past several years and surveys continue to indicate that less than 25% of the public has significant confidence in their banks. The identification, recruitment, training and retention of qualified people to join such an unpopular industry presents a serious challenge and community banks cannot just plan on recruiting experienced management talent from other banks.

Regulators expressed an expectation [not a requirement] that both directors and officers of well-managed banks attend educational programs and suggested your bank document such individual participation.

Credit: Bank regulators expect boards to exercise effective oversight of loan policy, quality, concentrations and pricing. Regulators also expressed an expectation that well-managed community banks would have some system for stress testing their loan portfolios even though no such requirement [large banks only] has been forthcoming to date.

During our discussions, I expressed my view that bank directors are not credit officers and should not approve loans but rather focus on credit policy, loan pricing and concentrations. My firm's board advisory assignments over the past five years indicate that management at troubled banks frequently "delegated credit approval up" to the board and defended bad decisions with "the board approved the loan".

Interest Rate Risk: The significant decline in the value of bank securities portfolios in the second quarter of 2013 is a regulatory concern as many community banks have extended the maturities of their securities portfolios and added fixed rate loans during this period of historically low rates.

As community bank directors, you can expect continued regulatory focus on your management's stress testing of interest rate risk with the bank's asset liability model. Regulators indicated your bank's tangible capital is also an important ratio.

Cyber-Security: Discussions of cyber-security risk obviously included reference to the Target Store and other data security breaches. However, I was somewhat surprised by a regulatory discussion of the potential risk of online system disruption by governments that are not friendly to our country.

Community bank directors are expected to make certain that management has systems in place to monitor both internal data systems and those services provided by outside vendors. Regulators also indicated they expect community bank boards to provide oversight of the potential reputational risk associated with such a data breach.

Compliance: As expected, this is a top agenda item with regulators expressing a zero tolerance for violations. However, even bank regulators recognize that bank directors cannot spend all their board time reviewing compliance reports but they do expect you to have an effective internal compliance program.

In my view, compliance is just a regulatory 'given' – its like breathing, you just do it. However, time allocated to compliance is not an excuse for neglecting your other board oversight responsibilities such as capital, credit, management, earnings, interest rate risk, liquidity, etc. [CAMELS]

Strategic Risk: The Conference of State Bank Supervisors [CSBS] has partnered with the St Louis Federal Reserve Bank to undertake an ongoing study of Community Banking in the 21st Century. Their focus is to better understand the strategic challenges faced by community banks.

Your bank's strategic challenge [your bank's strategic plan] is to profitably provide essential financial services to your community's families and businesses in today's economic and regulatory environment. Not all community banks will survive and consolidation will continue; however, I continue to believe many community banks will prosper and even your regulators understand this will not be an easy task.

Directors Digest - 3Q 2014

Strategy & Risk Oversight

Balancing your bank's long-term growth strategy with appropriate risk oversight is a significant challenge for bank directors. This is a timely topic as strategic planning discussions typically take place this time of year when management presents their long-term plans and annual budget to your board for approval.

Developing a realistic growth strategy in today's slow growth economic environment is a tough challenge for the management of every financial institution. Avoiding the temptation to take excessive risk to enhance future earnings is a significant challenge. However, banks are in the business of managing risk, not avoiding all risks. So how does your board know when management has crossed the "risk" line?

Many articles have addressed board oversight of risk but designing a risk oversight system is not the first step. Your risk oversight system must be tailored to your bank's strategy and actual operations. One size of risk oversight does not fit all banks. This article presents a few personal observations based on my experience as a bank financial officer, bank board member and bank investor.

The key to profitable growth is a realistic strategy for offering competitive banking services in your bank's markets. The dramatic changes underway in how bank customers' access services presents a growing technological, marketing and competitive challenge.

Your board should make certain that management's strategic plan presents a candid view of your banks competitive strengths and weaknesses in your bank's markets. Make certain that management's plan specifically addresses existing and proposed loan services, deposit categories and other services your bank may offer. Acknowledge that banking is mostly a commodity business and loan and deposit offerings are essentially the same at all institutions.

Marketing strategy and staff training are essential to providing any competitive advantage within a commodity business. Bank managements frequently claim that "our people are our most important competitive advantage" - but just what is your management team doing to attract, retain and train the most competitive staff in today's rapidly changing marketplace?

Low pricing is not a strategy; it's a weakness that will damage long-term profitability. How does your management plan to grow and maintain appropriate margins?

Lowering credit quality standards to keep or "steal" business from a competitor is not a strategy; it's a weakness that can lead to excessive loan losses.

The most efficient firms in any commodity business, including banking, are typically the most profitable firms. Make certain that any costs designated as "investing in the future" have a real strategic purpose. Cost cutting is not a long- term growth strategy but maintaining efficient operations is essential to long-term profitability.

Prior to board approval of management's plan it's important to undertake a risk assessment to identify those areas that require policy discussions and detailed board oversight.

Does the plan require a significant increase in any specific existing or new loan category? Does projected loan growth create a concentration or pricing risk? Does your bank have the appropriate credit, technology and operational systems to manage the projected growth?

Does the plan project entering a new business? How does management plan to hire or train staff to manage the new business? Will the bank have the appropriate technology and operational systems to insure the business meets all compliance requirements?

Does the plan anticipate entering new markets and expanding its geographic footprint?

Why has management selected specific markets and what competitive advantage will the bank have following entry?

Do existing or proposed incentive compensation plans encourage excessive risk?

Just answering such questions during the planning process is not enough. The board must also establish an effective way to monitor results and future compliance with risk policy. Again, every bank has somewhat different challenges and one approach does not fit every bank.

I prefer a separate board risk committee to establish and monitor risk policy. Once the board has approved strategy the job of the risk committee is to look out the "windshield" in order to monitor trends and establish policy "curbs" to keep your bank "out of the ditch".

This is a different role than the audit committee. Audit has a full job in monitoring regulatory compliance, operational controls and the integrity of the bank's financial statements. In my view, these are very different roles.

Hopefully these thoughts will help provide you with a few ideas as you evaluate your bank's strategic plan and your board's risk oversight approach.

Directors Digest - 4Q 2014

2015: A Time For Strategic Action

Today's bank board agendas tend to be long on compliance and short on strategy. It's time for bank directors to shift focus from reacting to the swinging pendulum of ever increasing regulatory compliance and work with management to initiate strategic leadership to better serve their bank's customers and communities.

The pendulum of regulatory and compliance requirements is continuing to swing and this focus on compliance with both new and old regulations tends to dominate time on board agendas. Regulatory frustration is pushing many boards to consider selling to another institution. Investment bankers are urging boards to sell as the best alternative to maximize shareholder value. However, selling your bank may not be the best outcome for your shareholders, your customers and your community.

Small business provides most job growth and our nation's 5,600 community banks provide essential financial services to small business in communities, large and small, across our nation. As I have stated in numerous articles, our nations banking system provides the credit and liquidity required for economic growth. In simple terms, an engine won't run without oil and community banks provide the credit [oil] for economic growth in the communities we serve. Community banks have experienced NO net loan growth during the past seven years, a period when community bank boards have been reacting to increased regulation.

Your job as a bank director is to help guide your institution and leadership requires shifting your focus to strategic action, not just regulatory reaction. The following points should help guide your board agenda as we enter 2015.

People: Most experts say selecting the right CEO is the board's most important job; I disagree. I believe your board's most important job is to select, recruit and retain board members with the right skill sets required to provide appropriate guidance and oversight for management. The right board will select and retain the right CEO to lead your institution – poor boards lead to poor CEO selection.

Take the time as you enter next year to examine your board and make tough decisions if necessary; a bank director's job is too important to 'waste' a seat.

Strategy: Your management and board are best positioned to identify the needs of your community and your bank must be positioned to service those needs. Effective strategy is not a 'large binder' on the shelf; it requires effective focus and action.

> ***"If you don't know where you are going
> you might wind up someplace else"***
> ***Yogi Berra***

For many banks lacking a clear strategy that "someplace else" is down the road to sell the bank. Your job as a bank director is to make certain you have the right management team to design an effective strategy and deliver results.

Risk: Inadequate board focus on the strategic risk associated with past real estate related loan concentrations is now clearly apparent. Your board's challenge is to focus on strategic portfolio risk and not lose perspective by focusing on individual loan approval.

Board members are not loan officers and I continue to recommend that boards establish a risk committee to [1] evaluate investment, credit and funding policy, [2] review changes in asset concentrations and funding mix, [3] provide oversight over operating and technology risk, [4] monitor capital requirements and [5] NOT approve individual loans.

Compliance: Regulatory compliance is a 'given', it's like breathing, you just do it. As a result, I suggest you consider establishing a separate board compliance committee to provide oversight over regulatory risk.

Boards have had a tendency to assign every new element of risk oversight to the audit committee and, as a result, audit committees are over burdened today. Establishing a board level compliance committee would permit your audit committee to more appropriately focus on financial and accounting risk.

Future Actions: Unforeseen events will impact the annual plans and budgets you establish to achieve your strategic objectives.

> **"It's tough to make predictions,**
> **especially about the future."**
>
> **Yogi Berra**

The key to your bank's future success is having the right team and organizational structure to adapt your annual tactical actions so you achieve your strategic goals. Hopefully these thoughts help provide a few ideas for your next board agenda.

Directors Digest – 1Q 2015

Banking 101 & FinTech Competition

Too often it seems we forget the basics of banking in our increasingly complex world. Today's shift in financial services from our over-regulated banking system to less-regulated financial technology service providers [FinTech firms] is contributing to both disruptive competition and unintended economic consequences.

Banking 101 teaches us the fundamentals of credit and money creation. When your bank makes a loan the "proceeds" are created as new money and deposited in your customer's bank account – new money is created when your bank makes a loan. This newly created money is then redistributed by your customer to employees and suppliers, contributing to increased economic activity in your regional marketplace. The fundamental economic role of your bank is to provide credit and create money to support new economic activity.

However, community bank loan portfolios have simply not increased on a nationwide basis over the past six years. In fact, net loans outstanding for all banks between $100 million and $10 billion have decreased by $60 billion from $1.55 trillion in 2008 to $1.49 trillion last year. A lack of net loan growth results in no new money being created by community banks to support economic growth.

Small business has been the driver of economic growth and job creation for decades, and community banks are best positioned to serve the credit needs of small businesses in their local communities. The most recent Gallup Survey indicates that small-business owner optimism is improving but still below pre-recession levels. This low level of business confidence combined with increased regulation is contributing to soft loan demand. The relationship between this lack of loan growth to small business and our nation's soft and unbalanced employment recovery is inescapable.

The same money creation process is true for the Federal Reserve Bank – our central bank's purchases of government debt over the past eight years has been the nation's primary source of new money creation. However, much of this new money appears to have just boosted the value of financial assets rather than stimulate economic activity with substantial job growth.

Today we are witnessing a shift in financial services from our over-regulated banking system to less-regulated financial service providers. These new FinTech firms are gaining momentum; for example, they raised more than $5 billion in new investment from venture capital firms in 2014. New technology is enabling these less-regulated, non-bank firms to offer a wide range of bank-like payment and credit services at a lower cost to a wide variety of bank customers.

Banks and the Federal Reserve System have historically managed our nation's payment systems. The Durbin Amendment now limits bank interchange fees to the recovery of direct cost only with no contribution to overhead or profit. This limitation certainly eliminates the profit incentive for future development. It is not clear what impact the Durbin Amendment will have on the development of future payment systems.

Examples of new non-bank payment system competition include Apple and Bitcoin. I suggest you research both Apple Pay and Bitcoin if you are not familiar with these new technologies. As you know, regulators expect banks to police the payments system. However, new powerful technology has permitted Bitcoin to offer a fast, low cost and confidential method of transferring funds with a new unregulated virtual currency. However, Bitcoin's ability to secretly transfer funds that could be used to support illegal or terrorist activities is generating regulatory concern worldwide.

Non-bank development in credit services is also being boosted by technology. Traditional non- bank providers are being joined by new less-regulated startups such as Lending Club, Funding Circle and On Deck Capital. Lending Club's December 2014 IPO gave the company an $8.5- billion market valuation - higher than all but 14 of the largest U.S. banks.

From an economic viewpoint, if a non-bank lender borrows money directly from a bank to make and hold a new loan, then the non-bank lender's assets and funding increase and new money is created. However, when new loans generated by a non-bank lender are just sold [turnover of existing non-bank assets and funding] to banks or non-bank investors, then existing money is just being rearranged and no new money is being created to support economic growth.

On the deposit side, technology has enabled bank subsidiaries of national brokerage firms to consistently accumulate deposits; for example, Charles Schwab is now ranked #16 in size with $96 billion of deposits.

On the credit side, regulatory action is restricting consumer access to credit. For example, requests for tax refund anticipation loans are being shifted from banks to non-bank lenders such as Walmart, who recently announced plans to offer such loans to their customers.

The relationships between increased bank regulations, new technology, non-bank competition and customer demand is increasingly complex. However, increased bank regulation combined with new non-bank technology is clearly contributing to the rapid growth of new less-regulated [low-cost] non-bank providers. The ultimate impact of this disruption to the banking system's fundamental role of creating new money to support economic growth remains to be seen.

Directors Digest – 2Q 2015

Coping with Reality

No question – banks are today's favorite piñata of politicians, the media and many regulators; they all want to take a swipe. With no real letup in sight – what's a bank director to do?

Many articles, including a few by this author, discuss the unintended consequences of increasing regulation on the entire banking system and the impact of trickle-down regulation on community banks. Furthermore, it is important to recognize that regulators have yet to implement much of Dodd-Frank and the CFPB is just getting started.

However, in my view, today's focus on the regulatory burden is a distraction. My primary concern is not increased regulation; it's the negative public perception of all financial institutions by bank customers. According to the Gallup Survey, less than 25 percent of bank customers have a "great deal" of confidence in banking institutions, and 1 in 4 Baby Boomers are "dissatisfied." Today's reality is that we bankers are not popular and banks have not regained the trust of bank customers.

As bank directors, it is essential that we make certain our management team is focused on doing the right thing for our customers. We need to look at our services from the viewpoint of our customers – not just our accounting folks. Do our services and fees really appear to be understandable and fair? Would we bank with our institution if we were not directors? If not, why not? If yes, why?

Technology is rapidly changing how customers utilize financial services. Has your management briefed your board on the rapid shift to mobile banking? The delivery of financial services and the competitive landscape is also changing as less-regulated businesses utilize new technologies to offer non-bank credit and payment services. Has your management briefed your board on the impact that evolving non-bank competition will have on your institution?

The growing regulatory burden is today's reality in the boardroom, and any significant legislation that appears to aid any financial institution, including community banks, is unlikely to be enacted. As a result, trickle-down regulation will continue and the burden on community bank directors will continue to increase.

So, how do we cope?

Compliance with bank regulations is a given – we have no choice. Many regulations state that "management and the board shall" comply with a regulation with little or no distinction between the roles of management and the board. Regulators make it clear that directors are ultimately responsible if management fails to comply with any regulation.

Trickle-down regulation also involves risk management and stress testing, not just regulatory compliance. Community banks may not be subject to the same formal stress tests required of larger institutions. However, stress testing is a growing focus of regulatory oversight for community banks. We should all be familiar with how our asset/liability models simulate the impact of different interest rate forecasts on our institutions – in reality, a stress test. Similar stress testing for different credit scenarios, technology failure and operational issues is also evolving.

My suggestion for coping with your board's growing oversight responsibilities is to reexamine your board's committee structure to redistribute the workload. Would your board benefit from a board regulatory compliance committee to focus on regulatory compliance? The establishment of a board compliance committee could also permit your over-burdened audit committee to refocus on financial controls and audits. Would such a committee structure help your board focus more of its meeting time on your customers, current performance and future strategy?

My previous articles have addressed a variety of reasons why bank directors should not approve individual loans. History shows that credit concentrations sink banks, not individual loans. Bank boards are better served with a focus on the relationship between growth strategies and credit concentrations. Would your board benefit from a board risk committee that shifted focus from individual loan approval to risk oversight? Would such a board committee provide better and more coordinated oversight of credit, interest rate and operational risk oversight?

Coping with the growing regulatory burden is today's reality. I see no relief in sight and our challenge as bank directors is to manage our oversight responsibilities so we can truly focus on our communities, customers and the future of our institutions. Is it time to reexamine your board committees to determine what configuration best serves your bank?

Directors Digest – 3Q 2015

Read at Your Own Risk!

Board assessments are a hot topic this time of year and candor is frequently in short supply – especially when it comes to peer review and self-evaluation. Board assessments without individual candor are a waste of time. Providing your honest opinion of other board members' skills and performing a candid self-evaluation is the foundation for an effective board assessment.

The skill sets of individual bank board members needed to provide effective bank oversight continue to evolve. The starting point of an effective board evaluation is using a simple skill set matrix to identify the professional skills required of your bank's individual board members. If you haven't utilized this simple tool, you need to start today.

The following example lists the required skills down the left and board members [initials] across the top. Your goal is to identify what skills you need – not justify the skills you have on your current board.

The days are long past when your board's primary function was developing new business and approving loans. It's not whom you know but what you know that counts today. As a board member you have the essential responsibility to make certain your bank has the right board membership. Your management team also needs to help identify skill sets they believe are necessary for an effective board.

Board Skill	ABC	DEF	GHI	JKL	MNO	PQR
Finance			X			
Technology						
Marketing						
Legal	X			X		
Real Estate		X			X	

Once you develop and agree on the skill sets required, it's time to identify the skills you have and don't have on your board today. In addition, it's important to identify duplication – for example, as in the example above, do you have multiple attorneys or real estate developers? Do you have a "nice" or "legacy" person [PQR] on your board without any of the required skills?

Another hot topic today is board diversity including gender, age and length of service. For example, would your board benefit with the addition of a younger female with technology or marketing experience?

My experience indicates that smaller boards with the required skill sets are the most effective boards. As a result, duplication and lack of required skills wastes important board seats. My advice, don't utilize a skill set matrix if you don't have the courage to act.

The ever-growing regulatory burden makes it increasingly difficult to recruit qualified board members today. The American Association of Bank Directors has published a report that identifies over 800 rules and regulations that impact bank board members. However, your regulatory responsibilities make it even more important that you have the right mix of people and skills on your bank's board.

Now, why is the title of this article "Read at Your Own Risk"?

First, replacing a board member is certainly not fun. It's tough to ask a colleague to resign or not stand for re-election. Boards expect management to replace poor performers – it's easier to tell someone else they need to act than to do it yourself. However, boards have the same responsibility.

And you must ask yourself if you really provide an essential skill for your bank's board or is it time for you to depart? Maybe sharing this article will help current board members appreciate the importance of effective self-evaluation. However, my experience indicates that offers to resign are very rare.

Board members must work together as peers. We all have the same responsibility and liability – all votes are equal. Implementation of board changes is frequently stressful and produces hurt feelings. As a result, effective board leadership is required.

240

Sometimes a third-party assessment can be helpful – sometimes not. Boards generally recognize the changes that should be made but are just reluctant to act. A third-party can provide confidentiality of individual feedback and a reason to act, but don't request a candid appraisal if you are not prepared to act. Remember the old adage: Be careful what you wish for.

My challenge to you, as a bank board member, is for you to [1] challenge your board to undertake a candid board evaluation and [2] to look in the mirror and make an honest evaluation of your contribution to your bank's board.

Directors Digest – 4Q 2015

Board Insights & Scar Tissue

I plan to make this my last submission as a quarterly contributor to Directors Digest and want to share a few final insights from my experience as a board member, senior executive and investor over the past fifty years.

I have been fortunate to serve as a director of several community banks and corporations listed on NASDAQ and the NYSE. In every case the quality of financial performance was correlated with the quality of board leadership and the mix of professional skills brought to the table by individual directors. Anyone who has followed my board experience knows I have faced some very difficult situations and accumulated some scar tissue but I have also enjoyed working with some quality boards and extraordinarily talented people.

In my view the most important job of any board is having the courage to recruit and retain a balanced mix of people as directors. If you have the right people on your board you will also select an excellent CEO and have the courage to act if it's necessary to replace your CEO.

"Board Refreshment" and "Diversity" are the current buzzwords for board member recruitment. The media focus on the addition of women and minorities tends to emphasize ratios and overlook the skills and perspective required of new board members. Even as an "old pale male" I can agree that many boards today tend to look alike, duplicate skills and exhibit "mirror image" perspectives rather than represent the diverse range of skills and new perspectives needed to be effective.

Your toughest challenge is not adding new skills but replacing people, deciding when your board is best served by replacing an existing board member. Boards expect management to replace poor performers and fill each job by recruiting or promoting quality people. However, in my experience, it's really tough but necessary for directors to take the same actions at the board level.

Finally, ask yourself: Is it time for me to depart? In my case it is [age limit] and my job today is to help identify new directors that will bring better and more diverse skills to the table [hard to admit!] and improve the quality of the board.

Management Succession

It's a sad commentary on board leadership that so many companies, including many community banks, have no CEO succession plan. When carefully examined, the sale of many community banks due to "regulatory burden" is actually due to limited management depth and no meaningful CEO succession planning.

I have participated as a seller, buyer or financial advisor to billions of dollars of financial institution transactions. Many transactions are inevitable and although shareholders have benefited I am not proud of the negative impact that some of these transactions have had on loyal employees, bank customers and the local communities.

Community banks are the financial heart of many communities and "out of town" ownership is never the same. Is your board acting to insure that your institution has both the financial performance and management depth to at least have the option to remain independent?

"The Future Ain't What It Used To Be."
Yogi Berra

Without question, we are currently facing economic challenges that include low interest rates, slow economic growth and increasing market volatility. Looking back over the past fifty years we see that many financial institutions not only survived but excelled during a period that included several oil 'shocks', several wars, interest rates over 20% down to 0% [negative in Europe], several credit cycles and the worst recession since the 1930's. Leadership [people] made the difference.

The future holds great technological promise combined with growing cyber risk. New encrypted systems like the decentralized blockchain could be as disruptive as the Internet. The old marketing mindset will not work with future customers but credit risk and interest rate risk will continue to end the careers of future bankers. New executives [its different this time] seem to enjoy repeating the mistakes of the past. One of your jobs as a director is to help management to avoid repeating mistakes.

So in conclusion, I believe the one characteristic that has served me best has been a willingness to search out smart people, ask questions and listen. I am not the smartest person in the room but I am very fortunate to enjoy the friendship of many exceptional people and am thankful to have benefited from their knowledge.

"You've got to be very careful if you don't know where you are going, because you might not get there."

Yogi Berra

SECTION III

Personal Insight

Examples of each topic below appear throughout the previous chapters or in one of my articles. My objective in this final section is to provide a summery of my thoughts on each topic.

Leadership

Amazon lists over 180,000 books about leadership!

I am not going to attempt to explain how to become a great leader, as I don't think one size fits all. Remember, Churchill was considered a great leader during World War II but was voted out of office in peacetime. History shows that effective leaders have had many styles, personalities, backgrounds, etc.

I do believe it's important for a leader to be able to communicate a clear sense of mission or objective. Churchill clearly communicated a common objective that every UK citizen understood during the war.

The two most essential components of leadership in my view are mutual trust and respect. These attributes are earned, not learned.

I recall an example from my Navy Air training;

- A flight squadron leader has to trust that his squadron pilots respect his judgment and will follow him into battle – that they will protect his "back" [his life].

- The other pilots in the flight squadron have to trust and respect the judgment of their leader when they follow him into battle – their lives depend on his judgment.

The squadron leader obviously must know how to fly an airplane, and a business leader must understand their business and have the required business skills to be an effective leader. It's impossible to earn respect if you don't know what you are doing.

"Quality means doing it right when no one is looking"
Henry Ford

Effective leaders hire quality people and trust these people to do a quality job – effective leaders don't "micro-manage" staff. I expected my staff to know more about their job than I did – if I had to tell them what to do then I had the wrong person.

Mutual "respect" is a two-way street and includes respect for each person's talent, experience, opinions, gender, etc.

In my view, mutual trust and respect produce a team that works together in any organization; military, business, charitable and/or personal friends and family.

Plans, targets, budgets, mission are meaningless if you don't have a team that understands the objective and is committed to working together to achieve the objective.

This book contains numerous examples of effective leadership by CEO's that have produced excellent results. Each of these CEO's developed outstanding teams of people, and many of these people became effective leaders later in their own careers. The school of quality experience pays excellent dividends. For example, I see a pattern, what do you think?

- Vince Berta worked for David Grissom
- Pat Rusnak worked for Vince Berta

Finally, I don't believe the command and control method of leadership works. At Sunbeam, Al Dunlap was "in charge" and fear, not respect, was the dominant force. The results were catastrophic and ultimately bankruptcy.

The people described in this book have earned my trust and respect. Business ventures are not as serious as military battle but I believe life is too short to spend time and work with people you don't trust and respect.

"A sense of humor is part of the art of leadership, of getting along with people, of getting things done"

Dwight D. Eisenhower
President 1953 -1961

Tone at the Top

This description is an edited chapter from "It Is What It Is",
my previous book about saving AmericanWest Bank.

What separated AmericanWest Bank from the more than 300 other banks that failed during the financial crisis?

Leadership at every level made a difference. So a few observations on the bank's leadership in general and Pat Rusnak's [President & CEO] leadership style seem appropriate.

The "Tone at the Top" was visible and consistent. Rusnak's approach to dealing with problems was contagious; accept the facts ["It Is What It Is"], don't wallow in denial, don't waste time with the "blame game", identify and implement a solution.

Decisions were made - not deferred or avoided. Once the facts were clear Rusnak's decisions were implemented and supported. Management changes, closing branch offices, staff reductions, problem loan recognition, foreclosed property sales and other tough decisions were made promptly and communicated. This was true at all levels; the board, executive management and operating management. Bank employees got the message – authority for operating decisions was delegated down to the appropriate level - not delegated up to the CEO or the board.

Rusnak led by example – he was visible to other employees throughout the bank and no doubt word traveled that he worked as hard and as long [from his small office at the Support Center] as anybody in the organization. Frequent all-employee conference calls with Rusnak that included open questions and candid answers kept employees informed and engaged.

The board and Rusnak always kept an "open mind" and sought the best advice available. Rusnak didn't try to impress others with how much he knew; he asked questions and wanted to learn what others knew about a topic. He constantly spoke with a wide variety of people (bankers, attorneys, accountants, investment bankers, consultants and bank regulators) and consistently asked questions to learn more about the topic at hand.

The bank avoided corporate "perks" in an age of sacrifice. The bank had no company aircraft and Rusnak drove his own pickup truck, not a company owned luxury car. He didn't even have a reserved parking space. The negative reaction I have witnessed at other banks when tone-deaf corporate executives arrive in the company airplane or a company owned luxury automobile to announce expense cuts and employee layoffs did not occur at AmericanWest.

Past experience and mentors obviously played an important role. AmericanWest was fortunate to have the right person in the right place at a critical time. I have no doubt that seeing the example set by Vince Berta in Kentucky helped build a foundation for Rusnak's development. Berta was a beneficiary of his past relationship with David Grissom at Citizens Fidelity (as was I). Mentors make a difference and many people at AmericanWest will benefit in the future from their experience with Rusnak.

Qualified bankers are in short supply. I was very impressed throughout the past three years that Rusnak and his management team were not only able to retain talented employees but also attract talented people. Even in the toughest of times Rusnak kept a "can do" constructive attitude – "Tone at the Top" made a significant difference.

#   #   #

Many of the characteristics described above are consistent with the other leaders described in this book. Each has their own unique personality and approach but each sets the stage for success with their "Tone at the Top".

Global Markets & Competition

Amazon lists over 40,000 books on globalization! Much has been written, but I suspect not enough is understood.

Thomas Friedman's 2005 book, *The World is Flat*, describes the globalization of commerce in the twenty-first century, a condition we seem to accept and ignore at the same time.

This is not a new phenomenon, Citizens Fidelity completed every capital financing in the international markets. This book contains numerous examples that illustrate the impact global activity has had on my business career over the past fifty years.

Events in the Sunbeam chapter describe negative consequences related to management's failure in 1995 to adequately assess the impact global manufacturing would have on plans to expand Sunbeam's domestic manufacturing. Made in China now includes many quality products – not just cheap plastic items.

However, in my view, the most important aspect of globalization has occurred in the financial markets. We in the USA tend to have a domestic view rather than a global view. Any analysis of the 2007-2009 financial crisis indicates its global nature. What happens in the USA impacts Europe and vice versa.

Today the world's Central Banks have all adopted a low, zero or even negative interest rate policy in an unsuccessful effort to "kick-start" the global economy following the financial crisis.

The world has more money in circulation, but the velocity of money has dramatically declined on a global basis. I believe a widespread lack of confidence in global government policy prevents both consumers and business from spending and investing.

The low cost of borrowing has provided a unique opportunity for businesses of all types to acquire and consolidate operations to improve earnings with cost savings. However, this is not a recipe for economic growth.

Only time will tell, but I continue to believe that private business will continue to look for growth opportunities and company-by-company, the global economy will achieve modest growth.

The next question is; in what countries will growth occur? Government regulation and tax policy will play a significant role in every nation's ability to attract and grow private business.

Financial regulation is becoming more consistent across global markets. However, in my opinion, the combination of increased regulation and capital requirements on a global basis will curtail the global banking system's capacity to finance economic growth.

I suspect in a world of modest growth we should expect to see more competition between nations to attract and encourage private business. The current trend of domestic business to acquire an offshore company and relocate its corporate headquarters to the offshore location is an example of global competition by nations.

My advice to today's students who intend to become the next generation of business and governmental leaders is to learn more about global history and markets – competition for economic growth and jobs is worldwide. Even today professional jobs such as investment analysis, legal research, architectural design and technology development have been outsourced to professionals in other countries. Most likely the competition for your future job is not sitting in your classroom but instead is a hemisphere away.

Strategic Planning

Amazon lists over 75,000 books on strategic planning!

"[Planning] is not generally one road or another but the possibility of many different paths. If the choice were easy then the correct road would be clear. When the choices are difficult and the way ahead is marked by twists and turns then each step ahead is marked by opportunity, uncertainty and danger."

Mark Grant: "Out of the Box"

Navigating a small sailboat to a distant destination has been my analogy for strategic planning for a number of years. A frequent example has been planning a voyage from Florida to Bermuda – a voyage of opportunity, uncertainty and danger.

<u>First:</u> The sailboat captain/navigator determines the destination for the voyage – the goal is to safely reach Bermuda.

Strategic planning for a business requires the board of directors and chief executive officer to establish clear understandable strategic goals; earnings growth, asset growth, market share, etc..........

Note: I believe it is essential to focus on a few key goals that everyone can keep top of mind. I use a simple test; the goals are too complex if a manager is unable to go home and explain the goals to his/her spouse without notes.

"You've got to be very careful if you don't know where you are going, because you might not get there."

Yogi Berra

<u>Second:</u> The captain must have a qualified and experienced crew that can work together as a team to complete the voyage to Bermuda. Crewmembers need the knowledge to stand watch alone, stay on course, trim sails for efficient speed and call on their experience to ask for help when required.

The same is true for any business; you need qualified and experienced management in every position who can work together as a team to achieve your common goal.

A business requires a mix of experience and skills on its board of directors and on its management team to be most effective. A blend of talents provides better insight and perspective.

> *"The farther backward you can look,*
> *the farther forward you can see."*
> *Winston Churchill*

Third: Preparation of the sailboat for the voyage is essential. The captain must make certain that all the equipment [sailing, safety, etc] is the correct quality for an offshore voyage where weather and sea conditions can be very rough.

To compete, a business must also offer quality products and/or services to its ultimate customers. Remember the dog food story:

A classic business school case study describes the testing of marketing strategy for a new dog food with dog owners and pet stores. Based on this research the marketing programs and advertising were completed and the product was introduced.

Actual sales were a disaster – the dogs didn't like it!

> *"However beautiful the strategy,*
> *you should occasionally look at the results."*
> *Winston Churchill*

Fourth: The captain/navigator plots the planned course to sail from Florida to Bermuda. Multiple alternatives exist; sail the Northwest Passage through the Bahamas then head North to Bermuda, follow the gulfstream north along the coast and then head east to Bermuda, etc. The planned course must also avoid hazards such as shallow water or coral reefs.

Determining the planned course [strategy] depends on the long-term weather forecast. For example, a north wind at the start of the voyage would make the gulfstream dangerous, but provide a safe passage through the Bahamas.

This step is equivalent to selecting a competitive strategy to achieve the business goals, as any business must navigate through changing competitive and economic conditions.

Fifth: Long-term weather forecasts are not dependable and wind and sea conditions will change during the voyage. The captain/navigator will need to make tactical course adjustments; the course may change to accommodate a wind or current shift but the goal of safely sailing to Bermuda remains the same.

Long-term economic forecasts are also not dependable and competitive conditions are subject to change. Therefore, business is also required to adjust tactics to meeting changing economic and competitive conditions, but the goal [earnings growth] remains the same.

Sixth: The sailboats voyage to Bermuda is complete when it safely enters the harbor, but where does it go from Bermuda? Sailing is a never-ending voyage so long as the sailboat is sound and the crew is ready.

> **"You need to manage your business
> as if you will own it forever"**
>
> **Charles J Thayer**

The same is true for a business, strategic planning is a never-ending process designed to keep a company competitive with the right management team in place.

However, many businesses do reach a point that the sale of the business appears to be the best strategic alternative for its shareholders. But even in this case a business that has been managed well will achieve the best price for its shareholders.

> **"The future ain't what it used to be."**
>
> **Yogi Berra**

Financial Crisis Insights

*This final chapter is material edited from "It Is What It Is",
my previous book about saving AmericanWest Bank.*

One benefit of being the author of this book is the opportunity to share my own perspective and opinions throughout the text. This final chapter will address a few of the policy issues and <u>unintended consequences</u> that I believe contributed to the financial meltdown that occurred in 2007-2009.

As described in this section, government and regulatory policies frequently create considerable frustration for me. However, it's very important to make a clear distinction between regulatory policy and the people working at regulatory agencies.

I have spoken at numerous banking conferences across the country and this chapter reflects the issues I have addressed in many of those presentations.

I believe the following regulatory and governmental policies were significant contributing factors to the 2007-09 financial crisis; their combined impact turned what should have been a modest correction into a global liquidity, credit and capital catastrophe.

On the other hand, many individual bankers, bank boards and bank regulators have responded to a very difficult environment in a very positive manner. I remain confident that the financial system will once again be able to provide the financial fuel that is necessary for economic growth – despite monetary policy, congressional actions and bank regulatory requirements.

United States Congress

Housing Policy

Home ownership has been a key element of government policy for decades; "everyone should have the opportunity to buy his or her own home" has been a universal political philosophy.

Over the years multiple government programs at the federal, state and local government levels have been introduced to help people purchase their own homes, even if they could not afford to make a down payment. A whole new language developed: Option ARM, sub-prime, soft seconds, 120 loans, stated income loans, etc.

Freddie Mac and Fannie Mae, the two housing related Government Sponsored Enterprises [GSE] that failed in September 2008, became private market tools for government policy. Today they represent a $5 trillion taxpayer burden - the "elephant in the room" that has yet to be addressed by Congress.

The September 2008 financial meltdown can be traced to many factors, including Wall Street greed, but government housing policy provided the fuel for the sub-prime mortgage explosion and subsequent implosion.

The vast majority of community banks did not create nor participate directly in the sub-prime mortgage market.

However, when the mortgage music stopped on Wall Street, potential house buyers could not obtain a mortgage; home sales came to a halt; developers could not sell the lots they had developed; local builders could not sell the houses and condos they had built that had been financed by regional/community banks; companies that supplied labor and materials to the housing industry suffered; and community banks faced an increasing level of problem loans.

The mortgage crisis on Wall Street moved to Main Street.

Securities & Exchange Commission

2004: SEC Votes New Net-Capital Rules

This is the big one nobody discusses!

In a move in line with bank regulatory changes in Europe, the US Securities and Exchange Commission voted unanimously in an open meeting to approve new net-capital rules.

Goldman Sachs, Morgan Stanley, Merrill Lynch, Lehman Brothers and Bear Stearns are expected to apply soon to be designated as "consolidated supervised entities," or CSEs.

SEC Market Regulation Director Annette Nazareth told reporters after the meeting, "They are all very well-capitalized firms". In line with new capital adequacy standards coming into force soon under Europe's Basel accords, brokerages granted CSE status would be able to use in-house, risk-measuring computer models to figure how much net capital they need to set aside. Under Basel standards, some institutions could soon be cutting their net capital by as much as 50 percent.

SEC Commissioner Paul Atkins said monitoring the sophisticated models used by the brokerages under the CSE rules and stepping in where net capital falls too low "is going to present a real management challenge" for the SEC.

Since the new CSE rules will apply to the largest brokerages without bank affiliates, SEC Commissioner Harvey Goldschmid said;

"If anything goes wrong, it's going to be an awfully big mess."

An "awfully big mess" was an understatement! This capital policy change by the SEC in 2004 is what permitted the large investment banking firms to increase leverage from a maximum of 20x (5% capital) to over 40x (less than 2.5 %).

In volatile times, such as 2007-2009, market prices frequently moved between 1% and 2% a day – enough to wipe out a firm's entire capital account in a couple of days.

Basing the new Basel capital standards on in-house risk-measuring computer models was a policy blunder on a global scale that significantly magnified the liquidity and capital crisis of 2008 – just a few years later.

SEC: Bank Loan Loss Reserves

In 1999, the SEC accused SunTrust Bank of understating reported earnings by increasing the amount the bank allocated to their loan loss reserve. It should be noted the amount of the loan loss reserve is fully disclosed, it's certainly not a secret fund. SunTrust was forced to restate earnings as a result of the SEC's action and all banks were then forced to adopt loan loss reserve formulas based on historical experience.

With an expanding economy and years of minimal loan losses prior to 2007 these historical formulas dictated low loan loss reserves. As a consequence, bank loan loss reserves were inadequate to absorb the increase in loan losses as the economy entered the recession of 2007-2009.

The SEC's ill-advised action produced a rigid backward looking formula that assumed the good times would last forever and prohibited the banking system from being prepared for the 2007-2009 downturn in the business cycle.

Bank Regulatory Agencies

Bank regulators have a thankless job. They have no career upside if they even attempt to do something that might be viewed as helping the industry and they are subject to severe criticism if anything goes wrong.

Watching any Congressional hearing on TV clearly illustrates the toxic "blame game" in which they are expected to regulate our financial services industry. It must be tempting to regulate in anticipation of an Inspector General's final report, not for the good of the banking system or any individual bank.

Regulators stationed outside of Washington, DC, are expected to carry out policy, not make policy, so they have little if any flexibility. My experience with individual bank regulators across the country has always been positive – they are quality people attempting to do a professional job under very stressful circumstances.

However, I have experienced frustrating inconsistencies in the application of regulatory policy across the country. I attribute these inconsistencies to a lack of clear policy direction from Washington, DC.

Media reports based on interviews with selected bank executives often refer to cases of unnecessary loan write-downs and heavy-handed actions by regulators. Frankly, in the cases where Chartwell has played a role in such situations we have found regulatory action to be generally appropriate. As events unfolded in the 2007-2009 financial crisis, some bankers were simply caught as the "deer in the (economic) headlights."

It is essential for directors and bank executives at any troubled institution to build a professional and candid relationship with their regulators. Pat Rusnak at AmericanWest Bank not only understood this, but also did the best job of frequent and consistent communication with all the bank's regulators that I witnessed. Rusnak's practice was conveying "It Is What It Is" and the facts were communicated without any political "spin."

Having made the distinction between people and policy I will now share a few of my thoughts on the unintended consequences of regulatory policy that impacted troubled financial institutions during the financial crisis.

Regulatory Approvals: Management Changes

The time required for bank regulators to approve the promotion of an existing executive to a new position at a troubled bank – especially when that individual is to be the interim CEO – created unnecessary uncertainty.

Bank boards and management were expected to implement "prompt corrective action" without receiving "prompt regulatory approval" of their selection of new executive management.

This requirement also makes it very difficult for bank boards to recruit new qualified executives who were currently employed, as those executives were being asked to risk submitting their resignation before they obtained regulatory approval for their new executive position.

Regulatory Approvals: Executive Severance Payments

The requirement to obtain regulatory approval for the payment of any funds that bank regulators may deem to be severance created a significant dilemma for bank boards.

Troubled banks needed to downsize operations, and that included the need to downsize people – some jobs for good people simply needed to disappear. In my experience, such payments were seldom if ever authorized by bank regulators and this policy is very unfair in many circumstances.

In other cases, nonpayment just set up a legal dispute with terminated executives who had contractual rights, and created an expensive legal distraction for the bank. I concur that executives who were part of the problem should not receive severance – but labor law and the courts may not always agree.

Regulatory Orders: "Risk Adjusted" Capital Ratios

Regulatory policy concerning appropriate "risk adjusted" capital ratios was established in regulatory orders without publication, discussion or notification as the 2007-09 bank capital crisis unfolded.

"Well capitalized" banks were required to add capital. Published Consent Orders, that required capital ratios that were substantially above those required by FDICIA, became a proxy for a new regulatory policy.

Many community banks were required to increase capital ratios above "well capitalized" levels at a time when capital markets were closed. The only alternative open to them to increase capital ratios was to downsize their balance sheet by reducing the size of the loan portfolio.

The math is rather simple: when the market for new capital is closed, any regulatory requirement to increase minimum capital ratios by 1% creates the unintended consequence of reducing assets (loans) by 10%.

Banks across the country didn't know what bank regulators might require as a result at the bank's next exam. Even good banks were reducing loans at the very time elected officials were asking banks to make more loans to support the economy.

FDIC Policy: Liquidity & Brokered CDs

The unintended consequences created by the failure of the FDIC to approve the issuance of brokered CDs by "adequately capitalized" banks to replace maturing brokered CDs was one of the most disruptive policy decisions made during the financial crisis.

The banking system was experiencing a serious liquidity challenge and this FDIC policy contributed to the problem, not towards a solution.

FDIC: Deposit Insurance Fund

Media coverage consistently and incorrectly refers to the "Cost to the Taxpayer" when a bank fails. The FDIC Insurance Fund is a "self insurance" fund for the banking system supported by the premiums paid by banks. The FDIC is a government agency funded by the banking system – not by the taxpayer.

Funding policy for the FDIC Insurance Fund was counter-cyclical. No premiums were required when times were good and premiums were increased when credit problems were encountered. The banking system was required to pay more into the FDIC Insurance Fund when it could least afford to do so.

To compound the problem, troubled banks pay a risk-adjusted premium. Higher premiums for a troubled bank just reduce capital and increase the risk of failure.

FDIC: Deposit Insurance Coverage

The FDIC did this one right. Increasing the level of deposit insurance coverage was a significant step in helping restore confidence and in protecting liquidity for all banks.

U.S. Treasury: TARP & CPP

The Troubled Asset Relief Program, TARP, was introduced in October 2008 as an unworkable program to purchase troubled assets from banks. Fortunately, in January 2009, it was modified to include a Capital Purchase Program, CPP, to add capital to the banking system when none was available from the capital markets.

The delay in defining the rules, the uncertainty surrounding who qualified, and bad publicity related to its use for supporting AIG and other troubled institutions (including the auto companies) all damaged the reputation of the program.

When the CPP program was expanded to include community banks it provided a unique opportunity for many community banks to obtain capital "insurance" in a very uncertain economic climate.

TARP & CPP are consistently described as the "Wall Street Bailout". However, the TARP/CPP investments in financial institutions actually produced net cash gain of over $25 billion to the US Treasury as of June 2016.

On the other hand, the TARP investment in AIG had incurred a $10 billion cash loss as of June 2016.

The TARP investment in General Motors also produced a cash loss of $10 billion as of June 2016.

The public backlash against the "bailout" of Wall Street is an unfortunate "unintended consequence" of a program that arguably bailed out poor public policy at a net cash gain to the US taxpayer.

Financial Accounting Standards Board

Fair Value Accounting

The person who coined the name "Fair Value" for this accounting concept should get a "gold star" from his/her colleagues. It simply sounds un-American to argue against fair value – rather like disparaging the value of motherhood or apple pie. To their credit, bank regulators have voiced concern about the potential negative impact of fair value accounting for many years.

The introduction by FASB of expanded fair value concepts during the early days of the financial crisis was a significant contributor to the uncertainty that disrupted the financial markets. The precision of mathematical models to determine the market value of financial instruments that have no active market is questionable at best.

Fair value plays an important role for entities such as mutual funds or hedge funds that redeem investor funds from the fund itself. On the other hand, in my opinion, fair value has no place in the income statement of banks whose shares are traded between investors, not redeemed by the institution. This fundamental difference seems lost on the proponents of fair value.

Sufficient space is not available to discuss the many flaws of fair value accounting. However, if today's fair value accounting standards had been in place during the 20% interest rate environment of the early 1980's the asset write-downs due only to high interest rates would have resulted in the failure of nearly every bank in the nation. I fail to see how that outcome would have been in the best interest of investors or the citizens of our country.

Purchase Accounting

The FASB eliminated pooling accounting in June 2001 for all mergers; all future transactions were to be subject to purchase accounting treatment. I am not going to pass judgment on the technical merits of pooling versus purchase accounting - there were good arguments on both sides of the question.

However, an analysis of FDIC data indicates that purchase accounting added over $16 billion of goodwill to the financial statements of smaller regional and community banks ($1 to $10 billion asset size) over the nine years preceding the 2007-2009 financial crisis.

Goodwill impairment charges during 2008-2010 have reduced that amount by $10 billion. Goodwill would not have been recorded if these acquisitions had been completed with pooling accounting rather than purchase accounting treatment and such impairment charges would not have reduced bank capital during 2008-2010.

Furthermore, pooling required that acquirors could only issue common stock - no new debt could be issued to pay for a pooling transaction. An analysis completed by Chartwell indicated that, in the eight years preceding the 2007-2009 financial crisis, smaller regional and community banks had issued $50 billion of Trust Preferred Securities [TruPS], mostly through TruPS investment pools, to acquire other banks and repurchase stock.

This increase in TruPS issued by bank holding companies became a significant hurdle to many potential bank holding company recapitalizations [including AmericanWest] during the financial crisis.

United States Congress

The Dodd–Frank Act

Signed into law July 2010, the Dodd-Frank Act is intended to prevent another financial crisis. It includes 2,300 pages and 1,400 sections, requires 350+ new rules and establishes 7 new departments or agencies.

> *"If you have ten thousand regulations*
> *you destroy all respect for the law"*
>
> ### *Winston Churchill*

Only time will tell the total (positive and negative) impact the Dodd-Frank Act will actually have on the banking system.

Index of People

About the Author

Charles J Thayer is Chairman of Chartwell Capital Ltd., a firm that provides specialized advisory services to the board of directors and executive management of banks, corporations and institutional investors.

He is Chairman Emeritus of the American Association of Bank Directors [AABD] and served as Chairman from 2007 until 2013. The AABD is the national non-profit organization dedicated to serving the information, education and advocacy needs of financial institution directors.

Thayer serves as Lead Director of MainSource Financial Group [MSFG], a $4.0 billion banking institution with locations in Indiana, Illinois, Ohio and Kentucky. He was appointed to the board of directors of MainSource Financial Group and MainSource Bank in 2011.

He is designated as a Board Leadership Fellow by The National Association of Corporate Directors [NACD] and has served on the faculty for the NACD Masters Class. Thayer was a founding board member of NACD Florida in 2005 and he continues to serve as a board member.

Thayer has served on the board of trustees of the national Cystic Fibrosis Foundation, Washington, DC, since 1980. He served as Chairman of the Foundation's investment committee from 1993 to 2011 and as Chairman of Cystic Fibrosis Services, Inc., the Foundation's national mail order pharmacy, from 1994 to 2004.

He served on the board of the Louisville Development Bancorp [LDB] from 1997 until 2013. LDB's shareholders include Kentucky's major banks and corporations and LDB's banking subsidiary [Metro Bank] is dedicated to job creation and home ownership in the Louisville metro area.

He served on the boards of Republic Bancshares [NASDAQ] and Republic Bank, one of Florida's largest independent commercial banks, from 1999 until Republic was acquired by BB&T Corporation in 2004. Thayer served on the board of BB&T Bank [Florida] until July 2006.

CogenAmerica [NASDAQ], an independent power producer headquartered in Minneapolis, Minnesota, elected Thayer to its board of directors in April 1996. He served as a member of the Independent Directors Committee [IDC] until CogenAmerica's acquisition by Calpine Corporation in December 1999. The IDC was given full control of the acquisition process.

Thayer served on the board of directors of Sunbeam Corporation [NYSE] from 1990 until 1997. In January 1993 he was elected Chairman & CEO of Sunbeam, providing interim management until the election of a new CEO in August 1993.

Thayer had a twenty-year career in commercial banking prior to organizing Chartwell Capital in 1990. As Executive Vice President of PNC Financial [NYSE], Pittsburgh, he had management responsibility for finance, merger and acquisitions, investor relations, strategic planning, and he served as Chairman of PNC Securities Corp, PNC's capital markets subsidiary.

Prior to its acquisition by PNC in 1986, Thayer served as Executive Vice President and Chief Financial Officer of Citizens Fidelity [NASDAQ], Kentucky's largest banking institution.

Thayer is the author of "*It Is What It Is*" the book describing the recapitalization of AmericanWest Bank in 2010, has written numerous articles for a variety of banking publications and has been a frequent speaker at banking and corporate governance programs.

July 2016

Previous Books By Charles J Thayer

2010   *It Is What It Is*
        Saving American West Bank

1986   *The Bank Directors Handbook*; 2nd Edition
        Chapter: Asset/Liability Management

1983   *Bankers Desk Reference*
        Warren, Gorham & Lamont
        Chapter: The Financial Futures Market

1981   *The Bank Directors Handbook*; 1st Edition*
        Chapter: Asset/Liability Management

*Handwritten note inside of front cover:

*To my good friend Charles Thayer –
who climbed from the plains of Kansas
to the financial Olympics
in a decade of achievement!*

Maury Johnson

Acknowledgements & Disclaimer

My business career and an undertaking such as this book require family and friends willing to endure and tolerate obsessions and sacrifices. Frequently when was I was physically present I was absorbed in thoughts about business. This is a condition that has been tolerated by my family and friends over the past fifty years and I thank each of you and especially my wife, Molly, for your understanding.

The events and people described in this book are all based on my memory as my records for the past fifty years are not complete and in many cases no longer exist. I am certain others involved in these same events would provide differing descriptions, viewpoints and perspectives.

The descriptions of events, opinions expressed and any errors are mine alone.

" Thank You"

Charles J Thayer